THE
LETTERS AND WRITINGS
OF
GEORGE   FRIDERIC   HANDEL

THE
LETTERS
AND WRITINGS
OF
GEORGE FRIDERIC
HANDEL

Edited by Erich H. Müller

 BOOKS FOR LIBRARIES PRESS
FREEPORT, NEW YORK

First Published 1935
Reprinted 1970

STANDARD BOOK NUMBER:
8369-5286-3

LIBRARY OF CONGRESS CATALOG CARD NUMBER:
70-114882

PRINTED IN THE UNITED STATES OF AMERICA

PREFACE

THE number of letters and writings of George Frideric Handel which have up to the present become known to us is considerably smaller than that of any other musician.

These letters must form but a fraction of Handel's correspondence, and, at first sight, it seems strange that so few have been handed down to us. We must remember, however, that Handel did not, like many of his contemporaries, hold any office which would occasion the collecting of his records and writings. What has survived fortunately affords an insight into several sides of his life—into his family relations (the letters to Michaelson), in his work (those to Jennens), and in connection with his colleagues (those to Mattheson), and his friends (to Telemann) as well as distant acquaintances.

The present edition includes Handel's few prefaces, and his will. Orthography has been followed except in the case of Latin, which has been unified. If any examples of Handel's writing have escaped me, I must apologize and add that I should be grateful for information concerning them.

For friendly support and assistance I am indebted first to the Earl Howe, Dr. Ernst Foss and Mr. Westley Manning who set their still unpublished autographs at my disposal. Thanks are also due to the Victoria and Albert Museum, the late William Barclay Squire, and Dr. Ernst Weissenborn.

ERICH H. MÜLLER.

Dresden.

CONTENTS

CONTENTS

THE LETTERS AND WRITINGS
OF
GEORGE FRIDERIC HANDEL

I

To Johann Mattheson [1] in Hamburg

March 18, 1704.

. . . Ich wünsche vielmahl in Dero höchstangenehmen Conversation zu seyn, welcher Verlust bald wird ersetzet werden, indem die Zeit heran kömt, da man, ohne deren Gegenwart, nichts bey den Opern wird vornehmen können.

[1] Johann Mattheson was born at Hamburg, September 28, 1681. Coming from a wealthy family, he received a liberal education which developed his many-sided talents. He not only learnt to sing and to play nearly every instrument but also studied jurisprudence. In 1697 he appeared as a tenor at the Hamburg Opera House ; two years later he wrote an opera, *The Pleiades*, which he conducted himself from the harpsichord and in which he also appeared as a singer. On July 2, 1703, he became acquainted with Handel " on the Hamburg Mary Magdalene Organ." The young men quickly became friends and for some time Handel was a daily guest for dinner at the house of Mattheson's father. It was due to Mattheson's connections that Handel was admitted to the houses of Hamburg society and found music pupils. In 1703 the two friends together paid a visit to Dietrich Buxtehude in Lübeck, in 1704 Mattheson intended to make a journey to Holland, England, France and Italy, but he went only to Holland as his parents and friends, among them Handel, urged him to return. It is

Bitte also gehorsamst, mir Dero Abreise zu
notificieren, damit ich Gelegenheit haben möge,
meine Schuldigkeit, durch deroselben Einholung,
mit Mlle Sbülens [1], zu erweisen. . . .

known that in 1704 Mattheson quarrelled with Handel and
fought a duel with him, but they were later reconciled.
In 1705 Mattheson left the stage and entered the household
of the English ambassador as a tutor ; his duties took him
on different journeys with the ambassador. In the ensuing
years he was appointed secretary of legation and rose to
be provisional minister resident. In 1715 he was appointed Music Conductor and Prebendary in Hamburg
Cathedral. His hardness of hearing, which gradually
increased to deafness, compelled him in 1728 to resign his
position as music conductor. He died in Hamburg on
April 17, 1764.

[1] Mlle Sbülens is supposed to have gone with Handel
from Halle to Hamburg. Whether she was related to the
Sbüelen mentioned in letters XIV and XXI cannot be
ascertained.

2

II

(*To Andreas Roner*) [1].

(*End of July 1711*).

. . . Faites bien mes complimens à Mons. Hughes [2]. Je prendrai la liberté de lui ecrire avec la premiere occasion. S'il me veut cependant honorer de ses ordres, et d'y ajouter une de ses charmantes poesies en Anglois, il me fera le plus sensible grace. J'ai fait, depuis que je suis parti de vous, quelque progrés dans cette langue, &c.

[1] Andreas Roner was a German musician, settled in London, who became friends with Handel and corresponded with him. In 1730 he published a volume of psalms and hymns in English in imitation of Addison and John Denham, for a vocal part, violin and bass.

[2] John Hughes : b. Marlborough, January 29, 1677 ; he produced numerous historical and poetical works. In 1712 *Calypso and Telemachus*, an opera by Ernest Gaillard, was performed at the Haymarket Theatre, with a libretto by him. Presumably after his letter to Handel mentioned above, he sent the *Cantate of Venus and Adonis*. Of his poetical works intended for setting to music the following appeared in print : *An Ode in praise of Musick set for variety of Voices and Instruments* (London, P. Hart, 1703) and *Apollo and Daphne : a masque. Set to musick [by Dr. Pepusch] and perform'd at the Theatre Royal in Drury Lane London 1716.* Hughes was also a good violinist. He died in London, February 12, 1720.

3

III

To Mr. John G—— [cut away in MS.]

this 29 June 1716, London.

Sir

What Ever my Dividend is on five hundred
pounds South Sea Stock that The South Sea
Company [1] pays att the opening of their Books
next August pray pay Itt To Mr. Thomas Car-
bonnel or order and you will oblige

Sir

Your H   Servt

George Frideric Handel.

[1] The South Sea Company was incorporated in 1711,
and granted a monopoly of British Trade with South
America and the Pacific. In 1716, the date of Handel's
letter, the Company was in a very good way, having received further concessions, including a monopoly of the
slave trade with South America, in 1713 and 1716. In
1718 the King became Governor of the Company. The
famous Bubble burst in 1720, following some months of
hysterical speculation ; whether Handel still had his shares
then is not known.

4

IV

A Monsieur,
Monsieur Michael Dietrich Michaëlsen [1].
Docteur en Droit, à Halle, en Saxe.

à Londres,
ce 20 de Fevrier 1719.

MONSIEUR

MON TRES HONORÉ FRERE,

Ne jugez pas, je Vous supplie, de mon envie
de Vous voir par le retardement de mon depart,
c'est à mon grand regret que je me vois arreté
icy par des affaires indispensables et d'ou, j'ose
dire, ma fortune depend, et les quelles ont trainé
plus longtems que je n'avois crû. Si Vous
scaviez la peine que j'eprouve, de ce que je n'ai
pas pu mettre en execution ce que je desire si
ardemment Vous auriez de l'indulgence pour moy.

[1] Michael Dietrich Michaelsen : b. in Hamburg, 1680,
the son of the Royal Councillor and High-Bailiff Christian
Michaelsen. He became a Doctor of Law and War
Councillor, and was Lord of the manor and justiciary at
Eptingen. September 26, 1708, he married as his first
wife Handel's sister Dorothea Sophia. To secure her a
quiet life, since her health was not of the best, he bought
the estate of Stichelsdorf in 1718. There were five children
of the marriage : Christiane Felicitas, christened December 6, 1709, d. September 1, 1710 ; Johanna Friederike
(*cf.* p. 16, n.) ; Karl August, b. December 16, 1712,
d. December 21, 1714 ; Friedrich August, b. August 31,
1714, d. September 1, 1714 ; Emanuel Karl, b. October 15,
1716, d. July 4, 1720. Michaelsen subsequently married
twice (*cf.* p. 15, n., and p. 18, n.). He died July 20, 1748.

mais a la fin j'espere en venir à bout dans un mois d'icy, et Vous pouvez conter que je ne ferai aucun delay, et que je me mettrai incessamment en chemin, Je Vous supplie, Mon tres Cher Frere d'en assurer la Mama [1] et de mon obeissance, et faites moy surtout part encore une fois de Vôtre Etat, de celuy de la Mama, et de Vôtre Chere Famille, pour diminuer l'inquietude et l'impatience dans la quelle je me trouve, Vous jugez bien, mon tres cher Frere, que je serois inconsolable si je n'avois pas l'esperance de me dedommager bientot de ce delay, en restant d'autant plus longtems avec Vous. Je suis etonné de ce que le Marchand a Magdebourg n'a pas encore satisfait à la lettre de Change, je Vous prie de la garder seulement, et à mon arrivée elle serà ajustée. J'ay recus avis que l'Etain serà bientôt achemine pour Vos endroits, je suis honteux de ce retardement aussi bien que de ce que je n'ai pas pu m'acquitter plus tôt de ma promesse, je Vous supplie de l'excuser et de croire que malgré tous mes effors il m'a été im-

---

[1] Dorothea Handel : the mother of the composer. b. February 8, 1651, the daughter of the pastor Georg Taust of Diesskau and of his wife Dorothea, *née* Cuno. She married Georg Handel, April 23, 1683. George Frideric Handel was the second child. An elder son, born in 1684, died soon after birth. Further, there were two daughters, Dorothea Sophia (*cf.* p. 7, n. 1), b. October 6, 1687, and Johanna Christina, b. January 10, 1690, who died unmarried, July 16, 1709. Handel's mother died quite blind, December 27, 1730.

possible de reussir, Vous en conviendrez Vous
même lorsque j'aurai l'honneur de vous le dire
de bouche. Vous ne devez pas douter que je ne
haterai mon voyage : je languis plus que Vous
ne scauriez Vous imaginer de Vous voir. Je Vous
remercie tres humblement des voeux que Vous
m'avez adresses à l'occasion du nouvel'an. Je
souhaite de mon côté, que le Toutpuissant veuille
Vous combler et Vôtre Chere Famille de toutes
sortes de Prospèrités, et d'addoucir par ses pre-
tieuses benedictions la playe sensible qu'il Luy
a plu de Vous faire essuyer, et qui m'a frappè
egalement. Vous pouvez etre assuré que je con-
serverai toujours vivement le Souvenir des Bontés
que Vous avez eues par feue ma Soeur [1], et que
les sentimens de mà reconoissance dureront aussi
longtems que mes jours. Ayez la bonté de faire
bien mes Complimens à Mr. Rotth [2] et a tous

[1] Dorothea Sophia Michaelsen : Handel's sister, b. in
Halle, October 6, 1687. She married Michael Dietrich
Michaelsen in 1708 (cf. p. 5, n.). After a long illness
she died, August 8, 1718. From the funeral oration we
know that her consolatory text was " I know that my
Redeemer liveth." In *Messiah* (1742) Handel, in a charac-
teristic manner, assigned this text to a woman's voice.

[2] Magister Christian Roth : Handel's cousin, b. August
23, 1685, the son of the Halle conrector and later Leipzig
deacon Albrecht Christian Roth (d. December 10, 1701),
and of his wife Anna Eleonore Katsch (b. March 3, 1662,
d. December 6, 1695). He was made deacon of the
Moritz Church at Halle and church councillor of the
princely Saxon-Weissenfeld. He married, August 23, 1712,
Maria Sophia Limmer ; d. December 5, 1752.

7

les bons Amis. Je Vous embrasse avec toute Votre Chere Famille, et je suis avec une passion inviolable toute ma vie.

Monsieur

et tres Honoré Frere

Vôtre

tres humble et tres obeissant

Serviteur

GEORGE FRIDERIC HANDEL.

V

à Londres
Fevr. 24, 1719.

MONSIEUR,

Par la Lettre que je viens de recevoir de votre
part, datée du 21 du courant je me vois pressé
si obligeamment de vous satisfaire plus particu-
lierement, que je n'ai fait dans mes precedentes,
sur les deux points en question, que je ne puis
me dispenser de declarer, que mon opinion se
trouve generalement conforme à ce que vous avez
si bien deduit & prouvé dans votre livre [1] touchant
la Solmisation & les Modes Grecs. La question
ce me semble reduit a ceci : Si l'on doit preferer
une Methode aisée & des plus parfaites à une
autre qui est accompagnée de grandes difficultés,
capables non seulement de degouter les eleves
dans la Musique, mais aussi de leur faire con-
sumer un tems pretieux, qu'on peut employer
beaucoup mieux à approfondir cet art & à cul-
tiver son genie ? Ce n'est pas que je veuille
avancer, qu'on ne peut tirer aucune utilité de
la Solmisation : mais comme on peut acquerir les
mêmes connoissances en bien moins de tems par

[1] *Das beschützte Orchester, oder desselben zweite Eröffnung,*
worin nicht nur einem wirklichen galanthomme, der eben kein
Professions-Verwandter, sondern auch manchem Musico selbst
die alleraufrichtigste und deutlichste Vorstellung musikalischer
Wissenschaften . . . ertheilet. Hamburg 1717.

B

la methode dont on se sert à present avec
tant de succes, je ne vois pas, pourquoi on ne
doive opter le chemin qui conduit plus facilement
& en moins de tems au but qu'on se propose ?
Quant aux Modes Grecs, je trouve, Monsieur,
que vous avez dit tout ce qui se peut dire là
dessus. Leur connoissance est sans doute neces-
saire à ceux qui veulent pratiquer & executer la
Musique ancienne, qui a été composée suivant
ces Modes ; mais comme on s'est affranchi des
bornes etroites de l'ancienne Musique, je ne vois
pas de quelle utilité les Modes Grecs puissent être
pour la Musique moderne. Ce sont là, Monsieur, mes sentimens, vous m'obligerez de me
faire sçavoir s'ils repondent à ce que vous sou-
haitez de moi.

Pour ce qui est du second point, vous pouvez
juger vous même, qu'il demande beaucoup de
recueillement, dont je ne suis pas le maitre parmi
les occupations pressantes, que j'ai par devers
moi. Dèsque j'en serai un peu debarassé, je
repasserai les Epoques principales que j'ai eues
dans le cours de ma Profession, pour vous faire
vois l'estime & la consideration particuliere avec
laquelle j'ai l'honneur d'etre
Monsieur
votre tres humble & tres
obeissant serviteur
G. F. HANDEL.

VI

Preface to Handel's edition of the " Suites de pieces pour le Clavecin " [1]

(*London, November 14, 1720.*)
I have been obliged to publish Some of the following Lessons, because Surrepticious and incorrect Copies of them had got Abroad. I have added several new ones to make the Work more usefull, which if it meets with a favourable Reception ; I will Still proceed to publish more, reckoning it my duty, with my Small Talent, to serve a Nation from which I have receiv'd so Generous a Protection

G. F. HANDEL.

[1] Handel's most famous harpsichord work. The pieces may have been written as lessons for the princesses with whose musical education he had been entrusted by his patroness, the Princess of Wales. The best-known piece in the collection is the Air with Variations, popularly known as *The Harmonious Blacksmith.*

VII

TO THE
KING'S   *(London, end of 1720.)*
Most Excellent Majesty [1].

SIR,

THE Protection which Your Majesty has been graciously pleased to allow both to the Art of Musick in general, and to one of the lowest, tho' not the least Dutiful of Your Majesty's Servants, has embolden'd me to present to Your Majesty, with all due Humility and Respect, this my first Essay to that Design [2]. I have been still the more encouraged to this, by the particular Approbation Your Majesty has been pleased to give to the Musick of this Drama : Which, may I be permitted to say, I value not so much as it is the Judgment of a great Monarch, as of One of a most Refined Taste in the Art : My Endeavours to improve which, is the only Merit that can be pretended by me, except that of being with the utmost Humility,
SIR,
Your Majesty's,
Most Devoted,
Most Obedient,
And most Faithful
Subject and Servant,
GEORGE-FREDERIC HANDEL.

[1] George I.
[2] Handel's opera *Radamisto* was first produced at the Haymarket, April 27, 1720. The libretto was by Nicolas Haym.

VIII

(February 1725.)

To the Right Honourable The Lords Spiritual and Temporal in Parliament assembled.

The Humble Petition of George Frideric Handel sheweth That your Petitioner was born at Halle, in Saxony, out of His Majesty's Allegiance, but hath constantly professed the Protestant Religion, and hath given Testimony of his Loyalty and Fidelity to His Majesty and the Good of this Kingdom.

Therefore the Petitioner humbly prays That he may be added to the Bill now pending entitled 'An Act for Naturalising Louis Sechehaye'. And the petitioner will ever pray,

GEORGE FRIDERIC HANDEL.

IX

A Monsieur,
Monsieur Michael Dietrich Michaelsen,
    Docteur en Droit,
        a Halle en Saxe.

A Londres, ce $\frac{22}{11}$ *Juin 1725.*

MONSIEUR

ET TRES HONORÉ FRERE,

Encore que je me trouve tres coupable de n'avoir pas satisfait depuis si longtems a mon devoir envers Vous par mes lettres, neantmoins je ne desespere pas d'en obtenir Vôtre genereux pardon lorsque je Vous assurerai que cela n'est pas provenu de quelque oubli, et que mon Estime et Amitié pour Vous sont inviolables, comme Vous en aurez trouvé des marques, mon tres Honoré Frere, dans les lettres que j'ai ecrit a ma Mere.

Mon Silence donc, a ete plustôt un effêt de crainte de Vous accabler par une correspondence qui Vous pourroit causer de l'ennuy. Mais ce qui me fait passer par dessus ces reflexions, en Vous donnant l'incommodité par la presente, est, que je ne scaurois pas être si ingrat que de passer avec silence les bontés que Vous voulez bien temoigner a ma Mere par Vôtre assistance et Consolation dans son Age avancé, sans Vous en marquer au moins mes treshumbles remer-

14

cimens. Vous n'ignorez pas combien me doit toucher ce qui la regarde, ainsi Vous jugerez bien des Obligations que je Vous en dois avoir.

Je me contenterois heureux, mon tres Cher Frere, si je pouvois Vous engager a me donner de tems en tems de Vous nouvelles, et Vous pourriez etre sur de la part sincere que j'en prenderois, et du retour fidel que vous trouveriez toujours en moy. J'avois cru de pouvoir Vous renouveller mon Amitié de bouche, et de faire un tour en Vos quartiers a l'occasion que le Roy [1] s'en va a Hannover, mais mes souhaits ne peuvent pas avoir leur effet encore, pour cette fois, et la situation de mes affaires me prive de ce bonheur là malgré que j'en aye, je ne desespere pas pourtant de pouvoir etre un jour si heureux, cependent, il me seroit une consolation bien grande, si j'oserois me flatter, que Vous me vouliez bien accorder quelque place dans Votre Souvenir, et m'honorer de Votre Amitié, puisque je ne finiray jamais d'etre avec une passion et attachement inviolable

Monsieur et tres Honoré Frere
Vôtre treshumble et tresobéissant Serviteur
GEORGE FRIDERIC HANDEL.

je fais bien mes treshumbles respects a Madame Votre Epouse [2] et j'embrasse tendrement ma

[1] George I.
[2] Handel's greetings are intended for his brother-in-law's second wife, Christiane Sophia, who died, aged 24,

15

Chere Fileule [1] et le reste de Votre Chere Familie, mes Complimens s'il vous plait a tous les Amis et Amies.

September 24, 1725. She was the daughter of a merchant, Friedrich Dreissig, and was married, January 28, 1722.

[1] Handel's niece, Johanna Friederika Michaelsen, was the second child of his sister Dorothea Sophia and Michael Dietrich Michaelsen, b. in Halle, November 19, 1711. Handel himself was present at her christening, November 23. She married Dr. Johann Ernst Flörcke (b. Jena, July 9, 1695) a university professor in his native town, later High Ecclesiastical Councillor, Vice-President at Gotha and lastly Royal Prussian Privy-Councillor, Principal of the Friedrich's University and professor in ordinary for jurisprudence at Halle. He died June 9, 1762, as a hostage of the city of Halle, at Nürnberg. They had five children, of whom four died young. Johanna Friederika died February 28, 1771.

X

A Monsieur
Monsieur Michaelsen
Conseiller de Guerre de Sa Majeste Prussiеñe.

a Venise ce 11 de Mars 1729.

MONSIEUR
ET TRES HOÑORÉ FRERE

Vous trouverez par la lettre que j'envoye icy a
ma Mere que j'aye bien obtenu l'hoñeur de la
Votre du 18 du passé.

Permettez moy que je Vous en fasse particu-
lierement mes remerciments par ces lignes, et que
je Vous supplie a vouloir bien continuer de me
donner de tems en tems Vos cheres nouvelles
pendant que je me trouve en voyage par ce pais
cy, puisque Vous ne pouvez pas ignorer l'interest
et la satisfaction que j'en prens. Vous n'avez
qu'a les addresser toujours à Mr Joseph Smith [1]
Banquier à Venise (coñe j'ay deja mentioñé) qui
me les enverrà aux divers endroits ou je me
trouverai en Italie.

Vous juge bien, mon tres Hoñoré Frere, du Con-

---

[1] Joseph Smith, b. 1682. About 1700 he went to Venice
as a merchant. He was a great collector of books and
objets d'art, a large portion of which came into possession
of the British Museum. In 1729 he edited Boccaccio's
Decameron. From 1740 to 1760 he was English Consul at
Venice. In 1758 he married a sister of the Minister
Resident at Venice, John Murray. He died November 6,
1770.

tentement que j'ay eu d'apprendre que Vous Vous trouviez avec Votre Chere Famille en parfaite santé, et je Vous en souhaite du meilleur de mon Coeur la Continuation. la pensée de Vous embrasser bientôt me donne une vraye joye. Vous me ferez la justice de le croire. je Vous assure que c'a eté un des motifs principales qui m'a fait entre prendre avec d'autant plus de plaisir ce Voyage. J'espère que mes desirs seront accomplis vers le mois de Juillet prochain. En attendant je Vous souhaite toujours comble de toute prosperité, et faisant bien mes Complimens a Madame Votre Epouse [1] et embrassant Votre Chere Famille je suis avec une passion inviolable Monsieur

et tres Hoñoré Frere
Votre
treshumble et tresobeissant
Serviteur
GEORG FRIDERIC HANDEL.

[1] Here Handel's greetings are meant for his brother-in-law's third wife, Sophia Elisabeth Dreissig, who was a sister of his second wife. The marriage took place September 18, 1726.

XI

A Monsieur, Monsieur Colman,[1]
Envoyé Extraordare de S.M. Britannique,
aupres de S.A.R. le Duc de Toscane

a Florence.

Londres, ce $\frac{19}{30}$ de Juin, 1730.

MONSIEUR,

Depuis que j'ay eu l'honneur de vous ecrire, on
a trouvé moyen d'engager de nouveau la Sig^{ra}
Merighi [2], et cõme c'est une voix de Contr'Alto
il nous conviendroit presentement que la Feme

---

[1] Francis Colman was presumably acquainted with
Handel in England before he went to Florence. He wrote
the libretto of Handel's *Ariadne*, which was first produced
October 30, 1733, the birthday of King George II. He
was the father of George Colman, the dramatist. He died
April 20, 1734 (?) at Pisa.

[2] Antonia Margherita Merighi came from Bologna.
She was a contralto and as early as 1717 a virtuosa of
the Grand Duchess of Tuscany. From 1717 to 1721 she
sang in Venice, 1721 in Naples, and 1724 to 1726 again
in Venice. In 1729 she came to London, engaged by
Handel as " a woman of fine presence, an excellent actress,
and a very good singer." Her first part was Matilda in
Lotario, December 2, 1729. In 1730 she returned to Italy,
worked from 1732 to 1736 in Venice, and came again
to London in 1736, where she appeared at the Haymarket theatre ; she also sang in Handel's new opera
Faramondo. Her last part in England was in *Serse*, April,
1738.

19

qu'on doit engager en Italie fût un soprano.
J'écris aussi avec cet ordinaire a Mr. Swinny[1]
pour cet effet, en luy recomandant en meme
tems que la Femme qu'il pourra Vous proposer
fasse le Rolle d'home aussi bien que celuỷ de
Feme. Il y a lieu de croire que Vous n'avez
pas encore pris d'engagement pour une Femme
Contr'Alto, mais en cas que cela soit fait, il
faudrait s'y en tenir.

Je prens la liberté de Vous prier de nouveau
qu'il ne soit pas fait mention dans les Contracts
du premier, second ou troisieme Rolle, puisque
cela nous gêne dans le choix du Drama, et
d'ailleurs sujet a de grands inconveniens.
Nous esperons aussi d'avoir par Votre assistance
un home et une Feme pour la saison pro-
chaine, qui comence avec le mois d'Octobr
de l'anee Courante et finit le mois de Juillet
1731, et nous attendons avec impatience d'en
apprendre des nouvelles pour en informer la
Cour.

Il ne me reste qu'a vous reiterer mes assurances
de l'obligation particuliere que je Vous aurai de

---

[1] Owen MacSwinny : an Irishman who came to London
in 1706 to manage the Queen's Theatre, Haymarket. At
the end of the 1712–13 Opera Season he became bankrupt
and left for the continent with the takings of Handel's
Teseo. He lived for some twenty years in France and
Italy. In 1733, from Bologna, he put Handel in touch
with Carestini. Afterwards he returned to England ; d.
October 2, 1754, leaving his fortune to Peg Woffington.

votre Bonté envers moi a cet egard, qui ai l'honneur d'etre avec affection respectueuse
Monsieur
Votre
tres humble et obeissant.
Serviteur
GEORGE FRIDERIC HANDEL.

XII

A Monsieur, Monsieur Colman,
Envoyé Extraordinaire de S.M. Britannique,
aupres de Son Altesse Royale le Duc de Toscane
à Florence.

A Londres, $\frac{27}{16}$ de Octob^r, 1730.

MONSIEUR,

Je viens de recevoir l'honneur de Votre lettre du 22 du passée N.S., par laquelle je vois les raisons qui vous ont determiné d'engager Sr Sinesino [1] sur le pied de quatorze cent ghinées, a quoy nous acquiesons ; et je Vous fais mes tréshumbles remerciments des peines que Vous avez bien voulu prendre dans cette affaire. Le dit Sr Sinesino est arrivé icy il y a 12 jours et je n'ai pas manqué sur la présentation de Votre Lettre, de Luy payer a compte de son salaire les cent ghinées que Vous Luy aviez promis. Pour ce qui est de la Sig^{ra}

[1] Francesco Bernardi, known as Senesino, was born at Siena, about 1680. By 1719 he was singing at the Court theatre of Saxony and when Handel went to Dresden in search of singers he engaged Senesino for London. His first appearance was in November, 1720, in Bononcini's *Astarto*. His success was immediate ; this opera was followed by a revival of Handel's *Floridante*, then the composite *Muzio Scaevola*, and *Ottone, Flavio*, etc. With intervals caused by ill health and quarrels he sang for Handel until 1733. A further quarrel severed their connection and, after singing Italian Opera in Lincoln's Inn Fields for a season, he returned to Siena with a fortune. He died about 1750.

Pisani [1], nous ne l'avons pas eüe, et comme la saison est fort avancée et qu'on coṁencera bientôt les opéras, nous nous passerons cette année cy d'une autre Feṁe d'Italie, ayant déja disposé les Operas pour la Compagnie que nous avons presentement.

Je Vous suis pourtant tres obligé d'avoir songé a la Sig[ra] Madalena Pieri [2], en cas que nous eussions eu absolument besoin d'une autre Femme qui acte en homme, mais nous nous contenterons des cinq Personnages, ayant actuellement trouvé de quoy suppleer au reste.

C'est a Votre genereuse assistance que la Cour et la Noblesse devront en partie la satisfaction d'avoir presentement une Compagnie a leur gré, en sorte qu'il ne me reste qu'a vous en marquer mes sentiments particuliers de gratitude et a Vous assurer de l'attention tres respectueuse avec laquelle j'ay l'honneur d'etre, Monsieur

Votre
treshumble et tresobéissant serviteur
GEORGE FRIDERIC HANDEL.

---

[1] Nothing further is to be found about this singer.
[2] Maria Magdalena Pieri : sang in Naples in 1722 and was already virtuosa of the Duke of Modena. In 1726, 1729, and 1730 she sang in Venice.

XIII

A *Monsieur*
Monsieur Dietrich Michael Michaëlsen
Conseiller de Guerre de Sa Majesté Prussienne
  a Halle en Saxe.

London den $\frac{23}{12}$ February *1731*.

MONSIEUR
  ET TRES HONORÉ FRERE.

Deroselben geEhrtestes vom 6. January habe zurecht erhalten, woraus mit mehreren ersehen die Sorgfalt die Derselbe genom̄en meine Seelige Fr. Mutter gesiemend und Ihrem letzten Willen gemäss zur Erde zu bestatten. Ich kann nicht umhin allhier meine Thränen fliessen zu lassen. Doch es hat dem Höchsten also gefallen, Dessen heyligen Willen mit Christlicher Gelassenheit mich unterwerffe. Ihr Gedächtniss wird indessen nim̄er bey mir erlöschen, bisz wier nach diesem Leben wieder vereiniget werden, welches der Grundgütige Gott in Genaden verleyhen wolle. Die vielfältige Obligationes so ich meinem HochgeEhrten HEn Bruder habe vor die beständige Treüe und Sorgfalt womit Derselbe meiner lieben Seeligen Frau Mutter allezeit assitiret werde nicht mit Worten allein sondern mit schuldiger Erkäntlichkeit zu bezeügen mir vorbehalten. Ich verhoffe, dasz Mhhhl Bruder mein letzteres so in Antwort auff dessen vom 28. Decembris a.p. geschrieben, mit den Inlagen an den HEn

24

GEORGE FRIDERIC HANDEL

Consistorial Rath Franck [1] und HEn Vetter
Diaconus Taust [2] wird zurecht erhalten haben.
Erwarte also mit Verlangen Dessen Hochge-
Ehrteste Antwort, mit angeschlossener Notice
wegen der auffgewandten Unkosten, wie auch
die gedruckte Parentation und Leichen Carmina.
Indessen bin sehr verbunden vor das letzt überschickte herrliche Carmen welches als ein hoch-
geschäztes Andenken verwahren werde.
Uebrigens Condolire von Hertzen Mhhhl Bruder
und Dessen HochgeEhrteste Fr. Liebste wegen
des sensiblen Verlustes so Sie gehabt durch das
Absterben dessen Herrn Schwagers [3] und bin
sonderlich durch dessen Christmässige Gelassenheit erbaut. Der Höchste erfülle an uns allen
dessen trostreichen Wunsch, in Dessen allgewalti-
gen Schutz meinen HochgeEhrten HEn Bruder
mit Dero gesamten liebwehrtesten Familie em-

[1] Johann Georg Franck : Royal Prussian Ecclesiastical
Councillor ; delivered the funeral oration over Handel's
mother, which appeared under the title : *Die Wohlthaten,
welche Gott, durch einen seligen Todt, an seinen Gläubigen thut
und sie dadurch erwecket nach denselben zu verlangen, Wurden in
dem, der weiland Wol-Edlen, Hoch-Ehr und Tugendbelobten
Frau, FRAU Dorotheen Taustin, des weiland Wol-Edlen und
Wolfürnehmen Herrn, Herrn George Händels . . . hinterlassenen
Frau Witwe . . . gehaltenen Leichen-Sermon vorgestelt.* 26 pp.
folio, printed by the Halle University and Council printer,
Johann Grunert.

[2] Johann Georg Taust : probably a grandson of the
pastor Georg Taust (d. 1685) ; since 1720 deacon at the
Laurenz Church at Halle a. S.

[3] Probably a brother of Michaelsen's third wife.

25

C

pfehle, und mit aller ersinlichen Ergebenheit
verharre
    Ewr. HochEdl.
       Meines HochgeEhrtesten Herrn Bruders
        treshumble et tresobeissant
          Serviteur
        GEORGE FRIEDRICH HÄNDEL.

XIV

A Monsieur
Monsieur Michael Michaëlsen,
Conseiller de Guerre de Sà Majesté Prussienne
   a Halle
      en Saxe.

a Londres ce $\dfrac{10\,d'Aout\ \ 1731}{30\ \ de\ Juillet}$

MONSIEUR ET TRES HOÑORÉ FRERE

Je vois par la Lettre que Vous m'avez fait l'honneur d'ecrire du 12 Juillet. n. st. en Reponse a ma Precedente, et par la Specification que Vous y avez jointe, combien de peines Vous avez prises a l'occasion de l'Enterrement de ma tres Chere Mere.

Je Vous suis d'ailleurs tres obligé des Exemplaires de l'Oraison Funebre que Vous m'avez envoyé et aux quels Vous avez voulu joindre un fait pour feu mon Chere Pere ; . . . Mr. Sbüelen [1].

Je scaurai apres m'acquitter en partie des obligations que je Vous ai. En attendant je Vous supplie de faire bien mes Respects et Compliments a Madame Votre Chere Epouse, a ma Chere Filleule, et au reste de Votre Chere Famille, et

---

[1] Johann Wilhelm Sbüelen : merchant. Nothing more could be found about him owing to the passage cut out of the letter. He died at Hamburg December 16, 1738 (*cf.* also p. 2, n.).

27

GEORGE FRIDERIC HANDEL

d'etre tres persuadé Vous meme, que je suis avec une passion inviolable.

    Monsieur
        et tres Honoré Frere,
            Votre (tres humble et tres obéissant
                Serviteur
                GEORGE FRIDERIC HÄNDEL)

XV

A Monsieur Monsieur Michael Dietrich Michaelsen Conseiller de
Guerre de Sa Majesté Prussienne
a Halle en Saxe.

London den $\frac{21}{10}$ *Augusti 1733.*

MONSIEUR ET TRES HOÑORÉ FRERE

Ich empfing dessen HochgeEhrtestes vom ver-
wichenen Monath mit der Innlage von unsern
liebwehrtesten Anverwandten in Gotha, worauf
mit dieser Post geantwortet. Ich freue mich von
Herzen desselben und sämptlichen Wehrtesten
Famille gutes Wohlseyn zu vernehmen, als dessen
beharrliche Continuation ich allstets anerwünsche.
Sonsten sehe die grosse Mühewaltung so sich mein
HochgeEhrtester Herr Bruder abermahl genoñen
wegen der Einnahme und Ausgabe vom vergan-
genen Jahre vom ersten July 1732 bis dreysigsten
July 1733, wegen meiner Seeligen Fr. Mutter
hinterlassenen Hauses [1], und muss mier meine
schuldige Dankbarkeit dessfals vorbehalten.

Es erwehnet mein HochgeEhrter Herr Bruder
dass es wohl nöthig wäre dass ich solches selbsten
in Augenschein nähmen möchte, aber, wie sehr
ich auch verlange denenselbigen Ihriges Orths
eine Visite zu machen so wollen deñoch der mier

---

[1] Probably the house " Zum gelben Hirschen " which
Handel's father had acquired in 1665 and which is still
pointed out as the supposed birthplace of Handel.

29

bevorstehende unvermeidliche Verrichtungen, so
mich gewiss sehr überhäuffen solches Vergnügen
mier nicht vergönnen, will aber bedacht sein
meine Sentiments dessfalls schrifftlich zu senden.
Es hat mein HochgeEhrter Herr Bruder sehr
wohl gethan sich zu erinnern meiner lieben
Seeligen Fr. Mutter letzten Willen wegen Ihres
Leichensteines zu beobachten, und hoffe dass
derselbe wird selbigen vollfüllen [1].

[1] The tombstone, which is no longer preserved, is said
to have borne the following inscription : *Zur sichern
Ruhestätte hat der vormalige H.F.S.M. auch Churf. Brandenburg
geheimder Cammerdiener, auch Leib-Medicus, auch 40jähriger
AmtsChirur-Herr Georg Händel 1674, diesen halben Bogen für
sich und die Seinigen zum Erbbegräbniss erkaufft und diesen Stein
zum Andenken hieher setzen lassen. Ist geboren hier in Halle von
Hn. Walentin Händel, Rathverwandter, 1622. den 24. Sept.
Sich verheirathet, 1643. mit Frau Annen, geb. Kattin, so Ao.
1682. den 9. Oct. selig verstorben, und hier bis zur fröhlichen
Auferstehung in ihrer Gruft in Gott ruhet. Hat in 40jähriger
Ehe mit ihr erzeuget 3 Söhne und 3 Töchter : als Dorothea
Elisabet, Gottfried L.M., Christooh, der in der Jugend verstorben,
Anna Barbara, Karl H.F.S. Weissenfels. Kammerdiener, Sophien
Rosinen ; davon erlebet als Grossvater 28 Kindes-Kinder u. 2
Kindes-Kindes-Kinder.—An. 1683. den 3. Apri ; sich zum
zweiten Mal verheirathet mit Jungf. Dorotheen Taustin, Herrn
Georg Taust, Senioris, wohlverdienten Predigers zu Giebichenstein
eheleibliche Tochter, in welcher Ehe er erzeuget 1 Sohn [? two
sons], Georg Friedrich, und [two daughters] Dorotheen Sophien,
Johanna Christina. Ist im wahren Glauben und an das theure
Verdienst seines Erlösers Jesu Christi 1697. den 11. Febr. selig
verstorben, und ruhet sein Körper allhier bis zur fröhlichen
Auferstehung aller Gläubigen.—Welche auch die allhier ver-
scharrten Gebeine seiner hinterlassenen Wittwe Frau Dorothea,
geb. Taust, als welche ihrem Eheherrn nach geführtem 33*

Ich ersehe aus der überschickten Rechnung dass de Fr. Händelin [1] so im Hause wohnet sechs reichsthaler des Jahres Stubenzins gibet, ich könte wünschen dass solcher ins künfftige Ihr erlassen werden möchte so lange als Sie beliebet darinnen zu wohnen. Ich übersende hierbey verlangter maassen die überschickte Rechnung von mier unterschrieben, meine obligation desfals werde gewiss nicht in vergessenheit stellen. Ich mache meine ergebenste Empfehlung an dero HochgeEhrteste Fr. Liebste. grüsse zum schönsten die wehrte Täustische Famille und alle gute Freunde. Ich werde bald wiederum meinem HochgeEhrtesten Herrn Bruder beschwehrlich fallen, hoffe aber, da ich desselben Gutheit kenne, dessfalls dessen pardon zu erhalten, ich bitte zu glauben dass ich lebenslang mit aller auffrichtigen Ergebenheit verbleiben werde Meines Insonders HochgeEhrtesten Herrn Bruders bereitwilligst gehorsamster Diener GEORGE FRIEDRICH HÄNDEL.

---

jährigen Wittwenstande 1730. den 27. Dezbr. der Seele nach in die Seel. Ewigkeit nachgefolget.

[1] Frau Händelin : perhaps the daughter-in-law of Handel's stepbrother Karl, who married his son George Christian Handel of Weissenfels, christened January 7, 1675, groom of the chamber to a Saxon prince.

XVI

(*To an unknown correspondent*)

London August 27, 1734

SIR

At my arrival in Town from the Country, I found myself honour'd of your kind invitation. I am very sorry that by the situation of my affairs I see my self deprived of receiving that Pleasure being engaged with Mr Rich to carry on the Operas in Covent Garden.[1] I hope at your return to Town, Sir, I shall make up this Loss. Mean while I beg you to be perswaded of the sincere Respect with which I am Sir

Your

most obedient and most humble

Servant

GEORGE FRIDERIC HANDEL

[1] Handel had for some years been producing operas with Heidegger at the King's Theatre, Haymarket ; this partnership was dissolved on July 6, 1734, in the most disastrous circumstances. Handel, who was at the time experiencing the most bitter opposition from the Prince of Wales and his party, opened in partnership with Rich in October. Covent Garden, which Rich was building out of the profits from *The Beggar's Opera*, was not ready until after Christmas, and the first operas of the season were therefore given at Lincoln's Inn Fields.

XVII

To Sir Wyndham Knatchbull [1], *Bart.,*
of Mersham le Hatch near
Ashford, Kent.

(*End of August 1734*).

SIR,

At my arrival in Town from the Country, I found my self honored of your kind invitation.

I am sorry that by the situation of my affairs I see my self deprived of receiving that pleasure being engaged with Mr. Rich [2] to carry on the Operas in Covent Garden.

I hope at your return to Town, Sir, I shall make up this loss. Meanwhile I beg you to be persuaded of the sincere respect with which

I am

Sir

your

most obedient and most humble

Servant

GEORGE FRIDERIC HANDEL.

[1] Sir Wyndham Knatchbull was presumably the 5th baronet of the name, who had married the daughter of James Harris of Salisbury, June 23, 1730. He died July 23, 1749.

[2] John Rich : theatrical manager, b. 1682 (?), the son of Christopher Rich, noted theatrical manager. On his father's death in 1714 he and his brother, Christopher Mosyer Rich, inherited the almost completed theatre in Lincoln's Inn Fields. He was the inventor of the English pantomime, of which he staged one every year from 1717 to 1760. First produced *The Beggar's Opera*, 1728. Built the Covent Garden Theatre and opened it in 1732, where he produced opera, plays and pantomimes. His daughter married Handel's great tenor, John Beard.

XVIII

*Monsieur Mattheson, secrétaire de
l'Ambassade britannique a Hambourg.*

A Londres. ce $\frac{29}{18}$ de juillet *1735.*

MONSIEUR,

Il y a quelque tems, que j'ay reçu une de Vos obligeantes Lettres ; mais à present je viens de recevoir votre derniere, avec votre ouvrage [1].

Je vous en remercie, Monsieur, & je vous assure que j'ay toute l'estime pour votre merite ; je souhaiterois seulement, que mes circonstances m'etoient plus favorables, pour vous donner des marques de mon inclination à vous servir. L'ouvrage est digne de l'attention des Connoisseurs, & quant à moi, je vous rends justice.

Au reste, pour ramasser quelque Epoque (de ma vie), il m'est impossible, puisqu'une continuelle application au service de cette Cour & Noblesse me detourne de tout autre affaire. Je suis avec une consideration tres parfaite, Monsieur,

Votre tres-humble et tres-obeissant Serviteur
G. F. HANDEL.

[1] *Die wohl-klingende Fingersprache, in zwölf Fugen, mit zwey bis drey Subjekten entworffen und dem Hoch-Edel-Gebohrnen, Hochgelahrten und Weltberühmten Herrn, Herrn Georg Friedrich Händel, Königl. Gross-Br. und Churfürstl. Braunschw. Lüneb. Capellmeister, also ein Merckmahl sonderbahrer Ehrbezeigung (gewidmet).*

XIX

To
   Mr. Jennens / Junior [1]
     at Gopsal near Atherstone
      Coventry bag.

London July 28/1735.

S^R

I received your very agreeable Letter with the inclosed Oratorio [2]. I am just going to Tun-

---

[1] Charles Jennens, b. 1700. He was a wealthy, well-educated lover of music, and enjoyed a reputation as a connoisseur. He joined Handel's circle of friends about 1735 and supported him faithfully at all times. Arranged Milton's *L'Allegro* and *Il Penseroso* and wrote a third part, *Il Moderato*, prepared the words of *Saul*, *Messiah*, and *Belshazzar* for Handel. According to Nichol's *Literary Anecdotes*, he, with Dr. Richard Bentley, the philosopher, is said to have suggested to Handel the idea of composing oratorios. In 1747 he inherited his father's estate at Gopsall, Leicestershire, and there, as well as at his town house in Great Ormond Street, kept great state and open house. He died unmarried November 20, 1773. His musical collection, including his organ (see letter XXVIII), was left to the Earl of Aylesford at Packington.

[2] To what libretto this refers cannot definitely be settled, but it is probably *Saul*, the first Jennens libretto that Handel used, though it was not produced until 1738. That the *Saul* libretto was from Jennens's pen is made clear by a letter from him to Lord Guernsey, dated September 19, 1738 (in the Aylesford family papers, first published by Newman Flower, *George Frideric Handel*, 1923), which throws light on Handel's activity in the summer of 1738 (*cf.* Flower, *op. cit.*, p. 251).

35

bridge, yet what I could read of it in haste gave
me a great deal of Satisfaction. I shall have
more leisure time there to read it with all the
Attention it deserves. There is no certainty of
any Scheme for next Season, but it is probable
that something or other may be done, of which
I shall take the Liberty to give you notice, being
extreamly obliged to you for the generous Concern you show upon this account. The opera of
Alcina [1] is a writing out and shall be send according to your Direktion, it is allways a great Pleasure to me if I have an Opportunity to show the
sincere Respect with which I have the Honour
to be
     Sir
       Your
          Most obedient humble
            Servant
           GEORGE FRIDERIC HANDEL.

[1] *Alcina :* first produced Covent Garden, November 6,
1736, in the presence of the Prince and Princess of Wales.

XX

To the Right .Honourable
the Earl of Shaftesbury [1]
A. Giles's.

London June 29th, 1736.

MY LORD.

At my return to Town from the Country
(where I made a longer stay than I intended) I
found myself honoured with Your Lordships
Letter. I am extremely obliged to Your Lordship for sending me that Part of My Lord Your
Fathers Letter relating to Musick [2]. His notions
are very just. I am highly delighted with them,
and can not enough admire 'em. Your Lordships kind remembrance of me makes me sensible
to the utmost degree, and it is with the pro-
foundest respect that I am

My Lord
Your Lordships
Most obedient and most humble servant
GEORGE FRIDERIC HANDEL.

[1] Anthony, fourth Earl of Shaftesbury, married first Lady
Susannah Noel, a daughter of Baptist, third Earl of Gains-
borough, March 12, 1724 (she died in 1758) ; second, March
20, 1759, Mary, the daughter of Viscount Folkestone. She
died on November 12, 1804. Shaftesbury d. May 27, 1771.

[2] The *Letter relating to Musick* by Anthony, third Earl of
Shaftesbury (1671–1713). He enjoyed a great literary
reputation on the continent, where Voltaire described him
as the greatest English philosopher, but his writings were
not in such favour at home. In 1709 he married Jane,
daughter of Thomas Ewer, of Lee, in Hertfordshire.

XXI

A Monsieur, Monsieur Michael Dietrich Michaelsen Conseiller de Guerre de Sa Majesté Prussienne a Halle en Saxe.

à Londres le $\frac{28}{17}$ d'Aoust 1736.

MONSIEUR ET TRES HONORÉ FRERE

Comme il ne me reste personne de plus proche que ma Chere Niece et que je vay toujours parfaitement aimée Vous ne pouviez pas m'apprendre une plus agreable nouvelle que celle qu'Elle doit epouser une Personne d'un Caractere et d'un merite si distingué. Vôtre seule determination auroit suffi pour la mettre au comble de son bonheur ainsi je prens pour un Effet de Vôtre Politesse la demande que Vous faitez de mon approbation la bonne Education dont Elle Vous est redevable assurerà non seulement sa félicité, mais tournerà aussi a Vôtre Consolation, a la quelle Vous ne dautes pas que je ne prenne autant de part qu'il se puisse.

J'ay pris la Liberté d'envoyer à Monsieur Son Epoux pour un petit present de Nopces une Montre d'Or de Delharmes avec une Chaine d'Or et deux Cachets un d'Amatiste et l'autre d'Onyx. Agreez que j'envoye dans cette même occasion pour un petit Present de Nopces a mà chere Niece l'Epouse, une Bague de Diamant d'une Pierre seule qui pese sept grains et demi et quelque peu de chose de plus, de la premiere Eau et de toute

38

Perfection. J'adresserai l'une et l'autre a Monsieur Sbüelen a Hambourg pour Vous les faire tenir. Les obligations envers Vous Monsieur et Madame Vôtre Epouse, que je Vous prie d'assurer de mes Respects, sont un point apart, dont je tacherai de m'aquitter à la première occasion. Permettez qu'apres cela je Vous assure qu'on ne scauroit etre avec plus de sincerité et de passion invariable que j'ay l'honneur de l'être Monsieur et tres Hoñoré Frere

      Vôtre

          tres humble et tres obeissant

          GEORGE FRIDERIC HANDEL.

XXII

To (Charles Jennens jr.)

Dublin Decem^{br} *29, 1741.*

S^R

it was with the greatest Pleasure I saw the continuation of Your kindness by the Lines you was
pleased to send me, in order to be prefixed to
Your Oratorio Messiah [1], which I set to Musick
before I left England. I am emboldened, Sir,
by the generous Concern You please to take in
relation to my affairs, to give you an account to
the Success I have met here. The Nobility did
me the Honour to make amongst themselves a
Subscription for 6 Nights, which did fill a Room
of 600 Persons. so that I needed not sell one
single Ticket at the Door. and without Vanity
the Performance was received with a general
Approbation [2]. Sig^{ra} Avolio [3], which I brought

[1] *Messiah* was composed by Handel in the almost in-
credibly short time of three weeks, between August 22 and
September 14, 1741. Early in November Handel travelled
to Dublin. There *Messiah* was produced for the first time
on April 13, 1742. The libretto was by Jennens's secretary,
Pooley.

[2] Handel's performances took place in Neal's Music Hall,
Fishamble Street. The first was *L'Allegro, il Pensieroso ed
il Moderato* on December 23, 1741.

[3] Sigra Avolio : sang with great success in the Dublin
performances ; the newspapers described her as " an
excellent singer." On April 13, 1742, at the first performance of *Messiah*, she shared the soprano part with

40

with me from London pleases extraordinary. I
have formed an other Tenor Voice which gives
great satisfaction, the Basses and Counter Tenors
are very good, and the rest of the Chorus Singers
(by my Direction) do exceeding well, as for the
Instruments they are really excellent. Mr. Du-
bourgh [1] being at the Head of them, and the
Musick sounds delightfully in this charming
Room, which puts me in such such spirits (and
my Health being so good) that I exert my self
on my Organ with more than usual success. I
opened with the Allegro, Penseroso, & Moderato,
and I assure you that the Words of the Moderato
are vastly admired. The Audience being composed (besides the Flower of Ladyes of Distinc-

Mrs. Cibber. Later she sang in *Messiah* in London, with
Mr. Clive, and others of Handel's works. She was the
first to sing *Let the Bright Seraphim* in *Samson*, 1743.

[1] Matthew Dubourg, b. 1703, son of the well-known
dancing-master Isaac Dubourg. Learnt to play the violin
at an early age and first appeared at Britton's famous
concerts ; shortly afterwards he became a pupil of Gemin-
iani. At the age of 12 he performed in public at the
Lincoln's Inn Fields Theatre and was billed already as
"the famous Matthew Dubourg." In 1728 he succeeded
Johann Sigismund Kusser as Master of the Viceroy of
Ireland's band. In addition to leading the orchestra on
this occasion for Handel, he also played in the Oratorio
oncerts given by Handel at Covent Garden, 1741-2.
in 1752 he succeeded Festing as Master of the King's
band, while retaining his post in Ireland ; d. London,
July 3, 1767. Several of his compositions appeared in
print.

tion and other People of the greatest quality) of
so many Bishops, Deans, Heads of the Colledge,
the most eminent People in the Law as the Chan-
cellor, Auditor General, &ct. all which are very
much taken with the Poetry. So that I am
desired to perform it again the next time. I cannot sufficiently express the kind treatment I
receive here, but the Politness of this generous
Nation can not be unknown to You, so I let
you judge of the satisfaction I enjoy, passing my
time with Honnour, profit and pleasure. They
propose already to have some more Performances
when the 6 Nights of the Subscription are over,
and My Lord Duc the Lord Lieutenant [1] (who
is allways present with all His Family on those
Nights) will easily obtain a longer Permission for
me by His Majesty, so that I shall be obliged to
make my stay here longer than I thought. One
request I must make to you, which is that you
would insinuate my most devoted Respects to
My Lord and My Lady Shaftesbury. You know
how much Their kind Protection is precious to
me. Sir Windham Knatchbull will find here my
respectfull compliments. You will encrease my
obligations if by occasion you will present my
humble service to some other Patrons and friends
of mine. I expect with Impatience the Favour
of your news, concerning Your Health and wellfare, of which I take a real share. as far for the

[1] William Cavendish, third Duke of Devonshire, K.G.,
Lord-Lieutenant of Ireland from 1737 to 1744 ; d. 1755.

News of your opera's, I need not trouble you for all this Town is full of their ill success, by a number of Letters from your quarters to the People of quality here, an I can't help saying but that it furnishes great Diversion and laughter. . The first Opera [1] I heard my self before I left London, and it made me very merry all along my journey, and of the second Opera, call'd Penelope [2], a certain noble man writes very jocosly, il faut que je dise avec Harlequin, nôtre Penelôpe n'est qu'une Sallôpe. but I think I have trespassed too much on your Patience, I beg you to be persuaded of the sincere veneration and esteem with which I have the Honneur to be

    S^r

      Your

         most obliged and most humble servant

              GEORGE FRIDERIC HANDEL.

---

[1] *Alessandro in Persia*, given on October 31, 1741, the music of which was composed of arias by Leo, Hasse, Arena, Pescetti, Lampugnani and Domenico Scarlatti. The libretto was written for Lucca by Francesco Vaneschi.

[2] *Penelope* was composed by Baldassare Galuppi. The libretto by Paolo Rolli. It was produced at the Haymarket Theatre on December 12, 1741, and was performed nine times in all.

XXIII

To
  Charles Jennens Esqr. Junior
    at Gopsal near Atherstone.
              Coventry bag

London Sept: 9th 1742.

DEAR SR.

It was indeed Your humble servant which
intended You a visit in my way from Ireland to
London. for I certainly could have given you
a better account by word of mouth, as by writing,
how well Your Messiah was received in that
country, yet as a Noble Lord, and no less than
the Bishop of Elphim [1] (A Nobleman very learned
in musick) has given his observations in writing
of this Oratorio, I send you here annexed the
contents of it in his own words—

I shall send the printed Book of the Messiah
to Mr Sted for you. As for my success in general
in that generous and polite Nation, I reserve the
account of it till I have the Honour to see you
in London. The report that the Direction of the
Opera next winter is comitted to my care, is
groundless. The gentlemen who have undertaken to middle with Harmony can not agree,
and are quite in a confusion. Whether I shall
do something in the Oratorio way (as several of

---

[1] Edward Synge, Bishop of Elphin 1742–62, son of
Edward Synge (1659–1741), Archbishop of Tuam.

my friend desire) i can not determine as yet. Certain it is that this time 12 month I shall continue my Oratorio's in Ireland, where they are agoing to make a large subscription allready for that Purpose.

If I had known that My Lord Guernsey [1] was so near when I passed Coventry, You may easily imagine, Sir, that I should not have neglected of paying my Respects to him, since you know the particular esteem I have for His Lordship. I think it a very long time to the month of November next when I can have some hopes of seeing you here in London. Pray let me hear meanwhile of your Health and Wellfare, of which I take a real share beeng with uncommon sincerity and Respect

> Your
>> most obliged humble Servant
>> GEORGE FRIDERIC HANDEL.

---

[1] Heneage Finch, Lord Guernsey, was up at Oxford in 1733 on the occasion of Handel's visit to that city, and read an oration before Handel in lyric verse on *The Praise of True Magnificence.* Later he became third Earl of Aylesford ; he was a relation of Charles Jennens and received a large quantity of Handel music—largely in Smith transcript—under Jennens's Will.

XXIV

(*To Charles Jennens jr.*)

London Juin 9th 1744.

DEAR SIR,

It gave me great Pleasure to hear Your safe
arrival in the Country and that your Health was
much improved. I hope it is by this time ferinly
establiched, and I wish you with all my heart
the continuation of it, and all the Prosperity.

As you do me the Honour to encourage my
Messiah undertakings, and even to promote them
with a particular kindness, I take the Liberty to
trouble you with an account of what Engagement
I have hitherto concluded. I have taken the
Opera House in the Haymarketh. engaged, as
Singers, Sigra Francesina [1], Mr Robinson [2], Beard [3],

[1] Elisabeth Duparc, called la Francesina. Came to
London from Italy in the late autumn of 1736 primarily
as a dancer. She soon danced before the Court, but after
that does not seem to have kept up her dancing. Does
not appear to have sung in public until Handel's *Faramondo*, January 7, 1738. Thereafter she sang consistently
for Handel. On January 10, 1741, she performed in his
last opera *Deidamia*, and thereafter continued to sing in
his oratorios.

[2] Turner Robinson also sang in the Haymarket Theatre
in 1744. Nothing more about him could be found.

[3] John Beard, b. London 1716 ; received his first musical
training as a chorister in the Chapel Royal under Bernard
Gates. Under his guidance in 1732 he appeared before
the public in the title part of Handel's oratorio *Esther* for

Reinhold [1], Mr Gates [2] with his Boyes's and

the first time as a singer. He soon became a favourite interpreter of Handel's works. As a stage singer he became popular in 1746 by his singing of J. E. Gaillard's well-known hunting song *With early horns*. In 1739 he married Lady Harriet Herbert, the widow of Colonel Herbert, who was the only daughter of Earl Waldegrave. She died after fourteen years of happy wedded life, aged thirty-seven. Beard was a highly cultured, artistic singer possessing a strong, expressive tenor voice. Six years later he married as his second wife Charlotte, daughter of the theatre director John Rich (*cf.* p. 33, n. 2). After his father-in-law's death in 1761 he became manager of Covent Garden Theatre. He retired from the stage in 1767, his last performance being as Hawthorne, a part he had originally created in Bickerstaff's *Love in a Village*. Deafness was added to his advancing age. Till 1776 he continued to sing in the annual performances of the New Year's Odes at St. James's palace. Rousseau, who heard him during his sojourn in London in 1766, confessed that he liked him best of all singers. Beard died at his country house at Hampton, February 5, 1791.

[1] Thomas Reinhold was born in Dresden about 1690. As a child he was consumed with a passion for music, which became centred in Handel whom he met at the house of the Archbishop who was reputed to be his uncle. He finally sought out Handel in London, where his first recorded appearance was in 1731. In 1737 he sang in Handel's *Arminio*, and in 1738 was one of the founders of the Royal Society of Musicians. He was also one of the original singers of *The Lord is a Man of War*. He died in Soho in 1751.

[2] Bernard Gates was born in 1685. By 1702 he was one of the children of the Chapel Royal; in 1708 he was made a Gentleman, in the place of John Howell. From 1740 to 1757 he was Master of the Choristers. The

several of the best Chorus Singers from the Choirs, and I have some hopes that Mrs Cibber [1] will sing for me. She sent me word from Bath (where she is now) that she would perform for me next winter with great pleasure if it did not interfere with her playing, but I think I can obtain Mr Riches's permission (with whom she is

children performed *Esther* at his house in James Street, Westminster, on February 23, 1732. The boys also sang the same work at a subscription concert at the Crown and Anchor Tavern and again at the rooms in Villiers Street, York Building. Gates left the Academy of Vocal Music in 1734 and took the Boys with him. He sang one of the airs in the first performance of the *Dettingen Te Deum* in 1743. He died November 15, 1773 at North Aston, near Oxford. Most of his work remained in manuscript.

[6] Susannah Maria Cibber was born in London, in February, 1714. She received her first musical training from her brother Thomas Augustine Arne. She made her debut in 1732, at the Haymarket, in Lampe's *Amelia*. In 1734 she married Theophilus Cibber, the son of Colley Cibber. Her mezzo-soprano voice was of slight compass and her knowledge of music according to Burney was not supposed to have been considerable ; nevertheless she had great power of expression and entranced the hearer with the emotional depths of her singing. She was the original Galatea in *Acis and Galatea*, and Handel wrote for her the air *He was despised* in *Messiah* with which she succeeded in making an indescribable impression. Later she concentrated entirely on acting and acquired a great reputation as a tragedienne. Quin was her ardent supporter when Garrick doubted, but afterwards those doubts were amply blown away, and when she died, in January, 1766— nine days after Quin—Garrick exclaimed, " Then Tragedy is dead on one side."

engaged to play in Covent Garden House) since so obligingly he has gave Leave to Mr Beard and Mr Reinhold.

Now I should be extreamly glad to receive the First Act, or what is ready of the new Oratorio [1] with which you intend to favour me, that I might employ all my attention and time, in order to answer in some measure the obligation I lay under. this new favour will greatly increase my obligations. I remain with all possible gratitude and Respect

    S^r

       Your

             most obliged and most humble

                    Servant

             GEORGE FRIDERIC HANDEL.

---

[1] *Belshazzar*, the first part of which Handel completed on July 30, 1744. The first performance took place in London on January 5, 1745.

XXV

To
Charles Jennens (Junior) Esqr.
at Gopsal
near Atherstone.
Leicestershire.

July 19, 1744.

DEAR SIR

At my arrival in London, which was Yesterday, I immediately perused the Act of the Oratorio [1] with which you favour'd me, and, the little time only I had it, gives me great Pleasure. Your reasons for the Length of the first act are intirely satisfactory to me, and it is likewise my opinion to have the following Acts short. I shall be very glad and much obliged to you, if you will soon favour me with the remaining Acts. Be pleased to point out these passages in the Messiah which you think require altering—

I desire my humble Respects and thanks to My Lord Guernsey for his many Civility's to me, and believe me to be with the greatest Respect
    Sr

        Your

            most obedient and most humble
                Servant
                GEORGE FRIDERIC HANDEL.

---

[1] See p. 49, n.

XXVI

To
Charles Jennens (Junior) Esqr.
at
>*Gopshall*
>>*near Atherstone*
>>*Leicestershire.*

London
Agosty 21
1744.

DEAR SIR

The Second Act of the Oratorio [1] I have received safe, and own my self highly obliged to You for it. I am greatly pleased with it, and shall use my best endeavours to do it justice. I can only say that I impatiently wait for the third Act and desire to believe me to be with great Respect
>Sr
>>Your
>>>most obliged and most humble
>>>Servant
>>>GEORGE FRIDERIC HANDEL.

[1] See p. 49, n.

XXVII

To
Charles Jennens (Junior) Esqr.
at Gopsal near Atherstone
Leicestershire.

London
Septbr. 13.
1744.

DEAR SR

Your most excellent Oratorio [1] has given me
great Delight in setting it to Musick and still
engages me warmly. It is indeed a noble piece,
very grand and uncommon ; it has furnished me
with Expressions, and has given me Opportunity
to some very particular Ideas, besides so many
great Chorus. I intreat you heartly to favour me
soon with the last Act, which I expect with
anxiety, that I may regulate my self the better
as to the Length of it. I profess my self highly
obliged to you, for so generous a Present, and
desire you to believe me to be with great esteem
and Respect
　　　Sr
　　　　　Your
　　　　　　　most obliged and most humble
　　　　　　　　　　　Servant
　　　　　　　　GEORGE FRIDERIC HANDEL.

[1] See p. 49, n.

XXVIII

To Charles Jennens Esqr. (*Junior*)
Gopsall
Leicestershire.

London
Octobr. 2.
1744.

DEAR SIR

I received the 3d Act [1], with a great deal of pleasure, as you can imagine, and you may believe that I think it a very fine and sublime Oratorio, only it is realy to long, if I should extend the musick, it would last 4 Hours and more.

I retrench'd already a great deal of the Musick, that I might preserve the Poetry as much as I could, yet still it may be shortned. The Anthems come in very proprely, but would not the Words (tell it out among the Heathen that the Lord is King) sufficient for one Chorus? The Anthem (I will magnify thee O God my King, and will praise thy name for ever and ever. (vers) the Lord preserveth all them that love him, but scattreth abroad all the ungodly. (vers and chorus) my mouth shall speak the Praise of the Lord and let all flesh give thanks unto His holy name for ever and ever Amen) conclude well the Oratorio. I hope you will make a visit to London next Winter. I have a good set of singers. S. Francesina

---

[1] See p. 49, n.

performs Nitocris, Miss Robinson[1], Cyrus, Mrs. Cibber, Daniel, Mr Beard (who is recovered) Belshazzar, Mr. Reinhold, Tobias, and a good Number of Choir Singers for the Chorus's. I propose 24 Nights to perform this season on Saturdays, but in Lent on Wednesdays or frydyas. I shall open on 3d of Novembr next with.............. yah ! I wish you heartily the continuation of your health, and professing my grateful acknowledgments for your generous favours, and I am with great esteem and Respect

    Sr

     Your

        most obliged and most humble servant

         GEORGE FRIDERIC HANDEL.

---

[1] Anastasia Robinson was born in Italy, 1698, the daughter of a portrait painter. She studied singing under Dr. Croft, Giuseppe Sandoni and " the Baroness." From 1714 to 1724 she was an opera singer in London, appearing in Handel's *Amadigi* in 1715. In 1723 she was married to the Earl of Peterborough, though he did not acknowledge her until the year of his death. He died in 1735, and after that Lady Peterborough was generally accepted. She died at Bevis Mount, Southampton, in 1750. She began her career as a soprano, but after a very severe illness her voice passed into a wonderful deep alto. Mrs. Delany describes her as follows : " of middling stature, not handsome, but of a pleasing modest countenance, with large blue eyes ; her deportment easy, unaffected and graceful ; her manner and address very engaging, and her behaviour on all occasions that of a gentlewoman."

XXIX

(*To Charles Jennens jr.*)

London. Sept. 30.
1749.

SIR

Yesterday I received Your letter, in answer to which I hereunder specify my Opinion of an Organ which I think will answer the Ends you propose, being every thing that is necessary for a good and grand Organ, without reed Stops, which I have omitted, because they are continually wanting to be tuned, which in the Country is very inconvenient, and should it remain useless on that account, it would still be very expensive althou' that may not be your consideration. I very well approve of Mr Bridge [1] who without any objection is a very good Organ builder, and I shall willingly (when he has finished it) give you my Opinion of it. I have referr'd you to

[1] Richard Bridge was one of the best organ builders of the eighteenth century. The oldest organ that can be proved to be by him is that of St. Bartholomew the Great, 1729. He also built organs in Christchurch, Spitalsfields (1730), St. Paul's, Deptford (1730), St. George's in the East (1733), St. Anne's, Limehouse (1741), Enfield Parish Church (1753), St. Leonard's, Shoreditch (1757) and in Eltham Parish Church. Together with Jordan and Byfield he built organ works in St. Dionys Backechurch, Yarmouth Parish Church and St. George's Chapel at Yarmouth. About 1748 he lived in Hand Court, Holborn. He died before 1776.

55

the Flute Stop in Mr Freemans Organ being excellent in this kind, but as I do not referr you in that Organ. The System of the Organ I advise is. Vizt

The Compass to be up to D and down to Gamut,
full Octave, Church Work,
One Row of Keys, whole Stops and none in halves.
Stops

An Open Diapason —	of Metal throughout to be in Front.
A Stopt Diapason —	the Treble Metal and the Bass Wood.
A Principal	— of Metal throughout.
A Twelfth	— of Metal throughout.
A Fifteenth	— of Metal throughout.
A Great Tierce	— of Metal throughout.
A Flute Stop	— such a one is in Freemans Organ.

I am glad of the Oppurtunity to show you my attention, wishing you all Health and Happiness, I remain with great Sincerity and Respect
Sir
Your
most obedient and most humble
Servant
GEORGE FRIDERIC HANDEL.

XXX

(*To the keeper of the Ordnance Office.*)

Saturdey
Febry 24
1750.

S<small>R</small>

I having received the permission of the Artillery Kettle Drums for my use in the Oratorio's in this season ; [1]

I beg you would conseign them to the Bearer of this Mr. Frideric Smith

I am

Your very humble servant

G. F. H<small>ANDEL</small>.

---

[1] This season was not a successful one for Handel. The kettle-drums must have made their appearance in *Theodora* which opened in March and ran but four nights.

E

XXXI

To Georg Philipp Telemann in Hamburg.[1]

à Londres ce $\frac{25}{14}$ de Decembr 1750.

MONSIEUR

J'etois sur le point de partir de la Haye pour Londres, lorsque Votre tres agreable Lettre me fut rendu par Mr Passerini.[2] J'avois justement le tems de pouvoir entendre chanter son Epouse. Votre Appuy et recommandation suffisoit a exiter ma curiosité non seulement, mais aussi a Luy

---

[1] George Philipp Telemann was born at Magdeburg on March 14, 1681. In 1700 he entered the University of Leipzig. He had trained himself so far in music that he was made organist of the Neukirche in Leipzig in 1704. In the same year he was appointed Capellmeister to Prince Promnitz at Sorau. In 1708 he went as Concertmeister to Eisenach and later became Capellmeister in the same town. Soon he was Musikdirektor at the Church of St. Catherine, Eisenach, while retaining his previous post and an appointment as Capellmeister to the Prince of Beyreuth followed. In 1721 he became Musikdirektor of the most important church in Hamburg. He died June 25, 1767. His reputation stood in the front rank during his lifetime but has sunk since. His fertility in composition was amazing, and Handel said that he could write a motet in eight parts as easily as anyone else would a letter. He got to know Handel in Halle and they often visited one another. In 1719 they met at Dresden.

[2] Passerini appeared in London in 1752 as a virtuoso on the violin and viola d'amore. Nothing is known of his wife.

58

accorder toute l'approbation, cependant j'étois bientôt convaincu moy meme de son rare merite. Ils s'en vont pour l'Ecosse, a remplir le devoir d'un Engagement qu'ils ont pour des Concerts, pendant une saison de six mois. Là Elle pourrà se perfectioner dans la langue Angloise, et alors (comm' ils ont intention a sejourner pour quelque tem a Londres) je ne manquerai pas de Leur rendre toutes les services qui dependront de moy.

D'ailleurs j'etois fort touché de Vos expressions polies et toutes remplies d'Amitié, Vos manieres obligeantes et Votre Reputation m'ont fait trop d'impression sur mon Coeur et sur mon Esprit, pour ne pas Vous rendre le Reciproque due a Votre gentile. Soyez sûr que Vous trouverai toujours en moy un retour plein de sinceritéet de veritable Estime.

Je Vous remercie du bel Ouvrage du Sisteme d'intervalle [1] que Vous avez bien voulu me communiquer, il est digne de Vos Occupations et de Votre Scavoir.

Je vous felicite de la parfaite Santé que Vous jouissez dans un Age assez avancé, et je Vous souhaite de bon Coeur la Continuation de toute sorte de prosperité pendant plusieurs Ans a l'avenir. Si la passion pour les Plantes exotiques & pourroit prolonger Vos jours, et soutenir la Vivacité qui Vous est naturelle, Je m'offre avec un

[1] *Das neue musicalische System*, which appeared in Mizler's *Musical Library*, vol. III, p. 713, in 1752.

sensible plaisir a y contribuer en quelque maniere. Je Vous fais donc un Present, et je Vous envoye (par l'adresse cy jointe) une Caisse de Fleurs, que les Connoisseurs de ces Plantes m'assurent d'être choisies et d'une rareté Charmante, s'il me disent le vray, Vous aurez des Plantes les meilleures de toute l'Angleterre, la saison est encore propre pour en avoir des Fleurs, Vous en serez le meilleur Juge, j'attens Vôtre decision la dessus. Cependant ne me faites pas languir longtems pour Votre agreable Reponse a celle cy, puisque je suis avec la plus sensible Amitie, et passion parfaite

Monsieur
Votre
tres humble et tres obeissant
Serviteur
GEORGE FRIDERIC HANDEL.

XXXII

à Londres ce 20 Sepr.
1754.

MONSIEUR

  Il y a quelque temps que j'ay fis preparer une
provision de plantes exotiques pour Vous les
envoyer, quand Jean Carsten le Capitain (a qui
je fis parler pour Vous les faire tenir) me fit dire
qu'il avoit apri que vous etiez defunt. Vous ne
doutez pas que ce rapport m'affligea extreme-
ment. Vous Jugeréz donc de la Joye que je dois
avoir entendre que vous vous trouvez en parfaite
Santé. Le meme Capitain Jean Carsten qui
vient d'arrive icy de retour de vos quartiers, me
mandes par un amy cette bonne nouvelle, et que
vous lui avoit Consigné une Liste de plantes
exotiques, pour vous les procurer, j'ay embrassé
cette occasion avec beaucoup de plaisir, et j'ay
eû Soin de faire trouver cettes plantes, et vous
les aurez presque toutes ; Come le Capitain
Carsten ne doit pas partir d'icy qu'au mois de
Decembre prochain, il, a bien voulû ce Charger
de les envoyer par le premier Vaisseau qui par-
tira d'icy, dont vous trouverez dans cet Billet
cy joint le nom du Capitain et du vaisseau. Je
souhaite que ce petit present que j'ose vous offrir
vous soit agreable ; Je vous supplié a me vouloir

61

donner des nouvelles de vôtre Santé que je souhaite trè parfaite, et toute Sorte de proscrité, qui
suis avec un estime inviolable,
Monsieur
      Vôtre tres humble et tres obeissant
      Serviteur
          G : F : HÄNDEL.

XXXIII

In the Name of God Amen.

I George Fréderic Handel considering the Uncertainty of human Life doe make this my Will in manner following

Viz.

I give and bequeath unto my Servant Peter le Blond [1] my Clothes and Linnen, and three hundred Pounds sterl. and to my other Servants a year Wages.

I give and bequeath to Mr Christopher Smith [2] my large Harpsichord [3], my little House Organ, my Musick Books, and five hundred Pounds Sterl.

[1] Nothing is known about Peter le Blond except that he died before March 22, 1757.

[2] John Christopher Smith, junior, was born in 1712, the son of John Christopher Schmidt of Anspach who came to England as Handel's Treasurer soon after the birth of his son. Christopher Smith showed a fondness and aptitude for music and was taught in turn by Handel, Pepusch and Roseingrave. He wrote several operas. He was the first organist of the Foundling Hospital, with which Handel was so closely associated. For many years he was Handel's chief amanuensis and, when Handel became blind, took down the last of his compositions from the composer's dictation. The MSS., which he received under Handel's Will he presented to King George III and they are now deposited in the British Museum. He died October 3, 1795.

[3] Possibly the Ruckers harpsichord, now in the Victoria and Albert Museum, South Kensington.

Item I give and bequeath to Mr James Hunter [1] five hundred Pounds Sterl.

I give and bequeath to my Cousin Christian Gottlieb Handel [2] of Coppenhagen one hundred Pounds Sterl.

Item I give and bequeath to my Cousin Magister Christian August Rotth of Halle in Saxony one hundred Pounds Sterl.

Item I give and bequeath to my cousin the Widow of George Taust [3], Pastor of Giebichenstein near Halle in Saxony three hundred Pounds sterl. and to her six children each two hundred Pounds sterl.

All the rest and residue of my Estate in Bank annuity's or whatsoever kind or nature.

I give and bequeath unto my Dear Niece Johanna Fridericia Floerken of Gotha in Saxony (born Michaelsen in Halle) whom I make my sole Exec. of this my last Will.

In wittness whereof I have here unto set my hand this 1 day of June 1750.

GEORGE FRÉDERIC HANDEL.

[1] James Hunter is not known.

[2] Christian Gottlieb Handel was a grandson of Handel's brother Karl, who was christened on September 30, 1649, and son of the Saxon prince's valet George Christian Handel, christened January 7, 1675. He was born at Weissenfels, January 9, 1714, and died in Copenhagen some time before August, 1757.

[3] Handel's aunt was the widow of the pastor Georg Taust, jr., who was, in 1683, a substitute pastor and from 1685 Pastor at Giebichenstein near Halle.

I, George Frideric Handel, make this codicil to my will.

I give unto my servant Peter le Blond two hundred pounds additional to the legacy already given him in my will.

I give to Mr Christopher Smith fifteen hundred pounds additional to the legacy already given him in my will.

I give to my cousin, Christian Gottlieb Handel, of Coppenhagen, two hundred pounds additional to the legacy given him in my will.

My cousin, Magister Christian August Roth, being dead, I give to his widow two hundred pounds, and if she shall die before me, I give the said two hundred pounds to her children.

The widow of George Taust and one of her children being dead, I give to her 5 remaining children three hundred pounds apiece, instead of the legacy given to them by my will.

I give to Doctor Morell [1], of Turnham Green, two hundred pounds.

---

[1] Thomas Morell was born at Eton, Buckinghamshire, March 18, 1703. On his father's death his mother kept a boarding-house at Eton. He was educated at Eton and King's College, Cambridge, after which he entered the church. He lived mainly at Turnham Green, where he had for neighbours Thompson, Hogarth, and Garrick. He died there February 19, 1784. With *Judas Maccabaeus* he became one of Handel's librettists. Later he wrote about it : " As to myself, great lover as I am of music, I should never have thought of such an undertaking (in which, for the reasons above, little or no credit is to be

gained) had not Mr. Handel applied to me when at Kew in 1746, and added to his request the honour of a recommendation from Prince Frederick. Upon this I thought I could do as well as some who had gone before me, and within two or three days carried him the first act of *Judas Maccabaeus*, which he approved of. ' Well,' says he, ' and how are you to go on?' ' Why, we are to suppose an engagement, and that the Israelites have conquered, I will have this,' and began working it, as it is, upon the harpsichord. ' Well, go on.' ' I will bring you more to-morrow.' ' No, something now.' ' So fall they foes, O Lord——' ' That will do,' and immediately carried on the composition as we have it in that most admirable chorus. The incomparable air, ' Wise man, flattering, may deceive us ' (Which was the last he composed. [This is a mistake by Morell. The air is only an adaptation of the song ' Se vuoi pace ' in *Agrippina*] as ' Sion now his head shall rise ' was his last chorus) was designed for *Belshazzar*, but that not being performed, he happily flung it into *Judas Maccabaeus*. N.B.—The plan of *Judas Maccabaeus* was designed as a compliment to the Duke of Cumberland, upon his returning victorious from Scotland. I had introduced several incidents more apropros, but it was thought they would make it too long, and they were therefore omitted. The Duke, however, made me a handsome present by the hands of Mr. Poyntz. The success of the oratorio was very great, and I have often wished that at first I had asked in jest for the benefit of the 30th night instead of a third. I am sure he would have given it to me ; on which night there was above £400 in the house." (Historical MSS. Commission, Report XV. Appendix, pt. 2.) Morell also wrote the libretto to *Alexander Balus*. In connection with it he relates the following anecdote : " The next year, he desired another (Oratorio) and I gave him *Alexander Balus*, which follows the history of the foregoing in the Maccabees. In the first part there is a very pleasing air, accompanied with the harp, ' Hark,

I give to Mr. Newburgh Hamilton[1], of Old
Bond-Street, who has assisted me in adjusting

hark, he strikes the golden lyre!' in the second two
charming duets, 'O what pleasure past expressing,' and
'Hail, wedded love, mysterious law.' The third begins
with an incomparable air in the affectuoso style, inter-
mixed with the chorus recitative that follows it. And as
to the last air I cannot help telling you that when Mr.
Handel first read it he cried out, 'Damn your iambics!'
'Don't put yourself in a passion, they are easily trochees.'
'Trochees, what are trochees?' 'Why, the very reverse
of iambics, by leaving out a syllable in every line, as
instead of "Convey me to some peaceful shore," "Lead
me to some peaceful shore."' 'That is what I want.' 'I
will step into the parlour and alter them immediately.'
I went down and returned with them altered in about
three minutes, when he would have them as they were,
and had set them most delightfully, accompanied with
only a quaver and a rest of three quavers." Further,
Morell wrote the libretti for *Joshua, Salomon, Theodora,* and
Jephtha, and translated *The Triumph of Time and Truth*
after the Italian original of Cardinal Pamfili. Also the
Oratorio *Nabal* produced at Covent Garden under Handel's
name in 1764, came from his pen; the music to it was
put together from different works of Handel.

[1] Newburgh Hamilton arranged Dryden's *Alexander's
Feast* for Handel, and wrote about it in the preface to the
libretto as follows : "The following Ode being universally
allow'd to be the most excellent of its kind (at least in our
language), all admirers of polite amusements have with
impatience expected its appearing in a musical dress equal
to the subject. But the late improvements in musick varying
so much from time to time, people despair'd of ever seeing
that affair properly accomplish'd : the alteration in the
words (necessary to render them fit to receive modern composition) being thought scarcely practicable, without break-

words for some of my compositions, one hundred pounds.

I make George Amyant, Esquire, of Lawrence Pountney Hill, London, merchant, co-executor ing in upon that flow of spirit which runs thro' the whole of the poem, which of consequence would be render'd flat and insipid. I was long of this opinion, not only from a difference in my own capacity, but the ill success of some ingenious gentlemen, whose alterations of, or additions to the original, prov'd equally ill-judg'd. But upon a more particular review of the Ode, these seeming difficulties vanish'd ; tho' I was determined not to take any unwarrantable liberty with that poem, which has so long done honour to the nation, and which no man can add to, or abridge, in any thing material, without injuring it ; I therefore confin'd myself to a plain division of it into Airs, Recitative, or Chorus's ; looking upon the words in general so sacred, as scarcely to violate one in the order of its first place : How I have succeeded, the world is to judge ; and whether I have preserv'd that beautiful description of the passions, so exquisitely drawn, at the same time I strove to reduce them to the present taste in sounds.— I confess my principal view was, not to lose this favourable opportunity of its being set to musick by that great Master, who has with pleasure undertaken the task, and who only is capable of doing it justice ; whose compositions have long shown, that they can conquer even the most obstinate partiality, and inspire life into the most senseless words.— If this Entertainment can, in the least degree, give satisfaction to the real judges of poetry or musick, I shall think myself in having promoted it ; being persuaded, that it is next to an improbability, to offer the world anything in those arts more perfect, than the united labours and utmost efforts of a Dryden and a Handel."

Hamilton also adapted Milton's *Samson Agonistes* for Handel.

68

with my niece, mentioned in my will, and give him two hundred pounds, which I desire him to accept for the care and trouble he shall take in my affairs.

In witness whereof I Have hereunto set my hand and seal, this sixth day of August, one thousand seven hundred and fifty-six.

GEORGE FRIDERIC HANDEL.

On the day and year above written, this codicil was read over to the said George Frideric Handel, and was by him signed and published in our presence.

THO. HARRIS [1].
JOHN HETHERINGTON.

I, George Frideric Handel, do make this further codicil to my will.

My old servant, Peter le Blond, being lately dead, I give to his nephew, John Duburk, the sum of five hundred pounds.

I give to my servant, Thomas Bramwell, the sum of thirty pounds, in case he shall be living with me at the time of my death, and not otherways.

In witness whereof I have hereunto set my hand,

---

[1] Thomas Harris was born in 1705. He was a brother of Joseph Harris. By his tailoring business and supplies for the army he had acquired considerable riches. He died September 23, 1782.

the twenty-second day of March, one thousand seven hundred and fifty-seven.

GEORGE FRIDERIC HANDEL.

On the day and year above written, this codicil was read over to the said George Frideric Handel, and was by him signed and published in our presence.

THO. HARRIS.
JOHN HETHERINGTON.

I, George Frideric Handel, do make this further codicil to my will.

My cousin, Christian Gottlieb Handel, being dead, I give to his sister, Christiana Susanna Handelin [1], at Goslar, three hundred pounds ; and to his sister [2], living at Pless, near Teschen, in Silesia, three hundred pounds.

I give to John Rich, Esquire, my great organ that stands at the Theater Royal, in Covent Garden.

I give to Charles Jennens, Esquire, two pictures, the old man's head and the old woman's head, done by Denner [3].

---

[1] Christiana Susanne Handel was born at Weissenfels, June 17, 1700.

[2] Rahel Sophia Handel, born at Weissenfels, November 6, 1703.

[3] Balthasar Dennar was born at Hamburg, November 15, 1685, and died April 14, 1749, at Rostock. Nothing further could be found about the pictures in question. He painted several portraits of Handel.

I give to (illegible) Granville [1], Esquire, of Holles-street, the landskip, a view of the Rhine, done by Rembrandt, and another, by the same hand, which he made me a present some time ago.

I give a fair copy of the score, and all parts of my oratorio called the *Messiah* to the Foundling Hospital [2].

In witness whereof I have hereunto set my hand, this fourth day of August, one thousand seven hundred and fifty-seven.

GEORGE FRIDERIC HANDEL.

[1] Probably Bernard Granville of Calwich, Derbyshire, and close friend of Handel, to whom James Smyth, another beneficiary under the will, wrote describing the funeral, see p. 72, n. 2.

[2] The Foundling Hospital, or " Hospital for the Maintenance and Education of Exposed and Deserted young Children," founded in 1738, was always dear to Handel. In May, 1749, he gave a performance of the Firework Music for the benefit of the Hospital and shortly afterwards he became one of the Board of Governors, where he joined his friend Hogarth. He also presented it with an organ, which he himself consecrated on May 1, 1750, when for the first time *Messiah* was heard in London. From then on he produced the work every year for the benefit of the house and regularly transferred to it £500. Handel's provision in his will bequeathing to the hospital the score and the voices of *Messiah* was prematurely known, and therefore the governing body endeavoured to derive from it the privilege of the sole production of the work and to have this confirmed by parliament, which aroused Handel's displeasure. Also the Organ Concert op. 7 Nr. 3 was, it is supposed, meant for a Foundling Hospital concert to take place in 1751.

On the day and year above written, this codicil was read over to the said George Frideric Handel, and was by him signed and published in our presence.

THO. HARRIS.
JOHN MAXWELL.

I, George Frideric Handel make this further codicil.

I give to the governors or trustees of the Society for the Support of Decayed Musicians and their Families [1] one thousand pounds, to be disposed of in the most beneficial manner for the objects of that charity :

I give to George Amyant, Esquire, one of my executors, two hundred pounds additional to what I have before given him.

I give to Thomas Harris, Esquire, of Lincolns Inn Fields, three hundred pounds ;

I give to Mr. John Hetherington, of First Fruits Office, in the Middle Temple, one hundred pounds ;

I give to Mr. James Smyth [2], of Bond Street, perfumer, five hundred pounds ;

[1] The Society for the Support of Decayed Musicians and Their Families was founded in 1738. Handel was among the first to become interested in it, and he continued to support it all his life. The first concert given to raise funds for the society was a performance of *Alexander's Feast*.

[2] James Smyth was present at Handel's funeral and wrote a long account of it to another of Handel's friends, Bernard Granville.

I give to Mr. Mathew Dubourg [1], musician, one hundred pounds ;

I give to my servant, Thomas Bramwell, seventy pounds additional to what I have before given him ;

I give to Benjamin Martyn [2], Esquire, of New Bond-street, fifty guineas ;

I give to Mr. John Belchar, of Sun Court, Threadneedle-street, surgeon, fifty guineas ;

I give all my wearing-apparel to my servant, John de Bourk ;

I give to Mr. John Cowland, of New Bond Street, apothecary, fifty pounds ;

I hope I have the permission of the Dean and Chapter of Westminster to be buried in West-minster Abbey, in a private manner [3], at the

---

[1] See page 41, n.

[2] Benjamin Martyn was born in 1699. He was the secretary of the company for the foundation of the colony of Georgia. In 1734 he was commissioned by the fourth Lord Shaftesbury to write a history of the first Lord Shaftesbury from the family papers. The work, however, was not successful. He had more success with his tragedy *Timoleon*. He died October 25, 1703.

[3] Handel originally wished to be buried in the Church-yard of the Foundling Hospital. However, according to his wish he was buried on Friday, April 20, 1759, in the south wing of Westminster Abbey. The funeral service, performed by Dr. Zachary Pearce, Bishop of Rochester, took place in the presence of more than 3,000 visitors. The choirs of the Chapel Royal, St. Paul's Cathedral, and Westminster Abbey sang the Funeral Anthem of Dr. William Croft.

discretion of my executor, Mr. Amyand ; and I desire that my said executor may have leave to erect a monument for me there, and that any sum not exceeding six hundred pounds, be expended for that purpose, at the discretion of my said executor.

I give to Mrs. Palmer, of Chelsea, widow of Mr. Palmer, of Chelsea, formerly of Chapel-street, one hundred pounds ;

I give to my maid-servants each one year's wages over and above what shall be due to them at the time of my death ;

I give to Mrs Mayne, of Kensington, widow, sister of the late Mr. Batt, fifty guineas ;

I give to Mrs Downalan, of Charles-street, Berkeley Square, fifty guineas ;

I give to Mr Reiche, Secretary of the affairs of Hanover, two hundred pounds.

In witness whereof I have hereunto set my hand and seal, this eleventh day of April, 1759.

G. F. HANDEL.

This codicil was read over to the said George Frideric Handel, and by him signed and sealed, in the presence, on the day and year above written, of us,

A. S. RUDD [1].

J. CHRISTOPHER SMITH.

[1] A. S. Rudd, a clergyman, died at Deal, May 6, 1757.

APPENDIX I

Letter from Aaron Hill [1] *to G. F. Handel.*

Dec. 5. 1732.

SIR,

I ought sooner to have return'd you my hearty
thanks, for the silver ticket [2], which has carried
the obligation farther, than to myself; for my
daughters [3] are both such lovers of musick, that
it is hard to say, which of them is most capable
of being charm'd by the composition of Mr
Handel.

Having this occasion of troubling you with a
letter, I cannot forbear to tell you the earnest-
ness of my wishes, that, as you have made such
considerable steps towards it, already, you would

[1] Aaron Hill was born in London, February 10, 1684/5.
He was educated at Barnstaple Grammar School and
Westminster, after which he went to Constantinople and
travelled in the Near East. He began to write in 1709,
and soon became interested in the stage and in 1709 is
said to have been " master of the stage " at Drury Lane.
He translated the libretto of *Rinaldo* which was produced
with enormous success at the Lane in 1711, during Handel's
first visit to England. " Although Hill was absurd and a bore
of the first water he was apparently a kindly and liberal
man, and abandoned the profits of his plays, such as they
were, to actors."—*D.N.B.*

[2] Season tickets engraved with the bearer's name were
issued by the theatres in various metals and ivory.

[3] Aaron Hill had nine children; three of his daughters
were named Urania, Astraea, and Minerva.

let us owe to your inimitable genius, the estab-
lishment of musick, upon a foundation of good
poetry ; where the excellence of the sound should
be no longer dishonour'd by the poorness of the
sense it is chain'd to.

My meaning is, that you would be resolute
enough, to deliver us from our Italian bondage ;
and demonstrate, that English is soft enough for
Opera, when compos'd by poets, who know
how to distinguish the sweetness of our tongue,
from the strength of it, where the last is less necessary.

I am of opinion, that male and female voices
may be found in this kingdom, capable of every
thing, that is requisite ; and, I am sure, a species
of dramatic Opera might be invented, that, by
reconciling reason and dignity, with musick and
fine machinery, would charm the ear, and hold
fast the heart, together [1].

Such an improvement must, at once, be last-
ing, and profitable, to a very great degree ; and
would, infallibly, attract an universal regard, and
encouragement.

I am so much a stranger to the nature of your
present engagements [2], that, if what I have said,
should not happen to be so practicable, as I con-

[1] Whether this letter had any bearing on the matter or
not, it was written just when Handel was giving up Italian
Opera in favour of Oratorio in English. *Esther* had been
produced on May 2, 1732, and was the first of the Oratorios.
[2] Hill had long severed his connections with the stage.

ceive it, you will have the goodness to impute it only to the zeal, with which I wish you at the head of a design, as solid, and imperishable, as your musick and memory.

        I am,

             Your most obliged,

             And most humble Servant

                   A. HILL.

APPENDIX II

TRANSLATIONS OF THOSE LETTERS APPEARING IN THE TEXT IN FRENCH AND GERMAN

I

. . . I should very much like to enjoy your pleasant conversation, and this desire will soon be satisfied when the time comes that your presence is found to be indispensable at the Opera. I also ask you humbly to inform me of your departure, so that I may have the opportunity of showing my respects by meeting you, together with Mlle Sbuelens. . . .

II

. . . Please convey my compliments to Mons. Hughes. I shall take the liberty of writing to him at the earliest opportunity. If, however, he would honour me with his commands, and if he would add one of his charming poems in English, he would give me great pleasure. Since I left you I made some progress in this language . . .

IV

Do not doubt, I beg of you, my willingness because of my delay in coming ; it is to my utmost regret that I am delayed here by the most pressing affairs on which, I dare say, my future will depend, and which have continued longer than I had expected. Did you but know how it pains me not to have executed that which I wish so ardently, you would give me your indulgence. But finally I hope to come to it in a month from now, and you may be assured that I will brook no delay and that I will travel without pause. Please, my dear brother, inform my Mama of this and assure her of my continued obedience, and also let me know once more how you are, how Mama is, and how your dear family is, in order to diminish the state of anxiety and impatience in which I find myself. You judge rightly, my very dear brother, that I should be inconsolable if I did not hope to remain the longer with you afterwards, and thus recompense me for this present delay. I am astonished that the merchant at Magdeburg has not yet honoured the draft. Please keep it and when I arrive it shall be put right. I have received news that the pewter will soon be on its way to you ; I am ashamed about this delay, and that I did not keep my promise sooner. I beg of you to excuse me and to believe that, in spite of all my efforts, it has been impossible for me to succeed. You will agree with me when I am able to explain it in person. You must not think that I shall dally on my journey ; I am longing to see you, much more than you can imagine. I thank you in all humility for the good wishes that you sent me for the New Year. For my part, I wish that the Almighty may shower prosperity on you and your dear family, and heal with his precious benediction the deep wound that he has chosen to inflict on you, which has affected me equally. I assure you that I shall always remember the kindness that you have shown to my dead sister, and that my gratitude will last as long as I live. Please be good enough to present my compliments to Mr. Rotth and to all our good friends. I embrace you and your dear family, and remain (etc. . . .).

V

From the letter which I have just received from you, dated the 21st inst, I find myself so far obliged to satisfy you more particularly than I have done in my preceding letters on the two points in question that I cannot but declare that my opinion generally concurs with what you have so well deduced and proved in your book on Solmisation and the Greek Modes. The question seems to me to reduce itself to this : whether one should prefer an easy and more perfect method to another that is accompanied by great difficulties capable not only of disgusting pupils with Music, but also of wasting much precious time that could be better employed in plunging deeper into this art and in the cultivation of genius ? It is not that I would put it forward that one cannot draw any use from Solmisation : but since one can acquire the same knowledge in less time by the method that is employed at present with just as much success, I do not see why one should not choose the route that leads *most* easily and in the shortest time to the desired end ? As to the Greek Modes, I find, Sir, that you have said all that there is to say. Knowledge of them is no doubt necessary to those who would practise and execute ancient music that has been composed according to these modes : but since we have freed ourselves from the narrow bounds of ancient music, I do not see of what use the Greek Modes can be for modern music. Those are, Sir, my sentiments, and you would oblige me by letting me know whether they are what you expected from me.

And for the second point, you can judge for yourself that it requires a great deal of concentration, which I cannot at present give to it on account of some pressing business that I have before me. As soon as I am a little more free, I will go over the principal epochs that I have had in the course of my professional life, to show you the esteem and particular consideration with which I have the honour to be (etc. . . .).

IX

Again I find myself very culpable in not having satisfied for so long my duties towards you by my letters, nevertheless I do not despair of your generous pardon when I assure you that this does not spring from any forgetfulness, and that my esteem and friendship for you are inviolable, of

which you will have found proofs, my very
honoured brother, in the letters which I have
written to my mother.

My silence, however, has been far more occa-
sioned by fear of overwhelming you with correspondence that might prove tedious to you. But
that which causes me to rise above these con-
siderations in giving you the presumption of this
present letter is that I cannot be so ungrateful
as to pass over in silence the kindness that you
have shown to my mother by your assistance and
consolation in her old age without at least sending you of my very humble thanks. You cannot be ignorant of the extent to which every-
thing regarding her touches me, and thus you
may judge well the obligations that I owe to
you.

I should count myself happy, my very dear
brother, if you would send me your news from time
to time, and you can rest assured of the sincere
interest that I would take in it, and of the loyalty
that you will always find in me. I thought that
I would be able to renew my friendship with you
personally, and to make a tour in your direction
when the King goes to Hanover, but my wishes
cannot be effected yet, this time, and the con-
dition of my affairs deprives me of this happiness ; but nevertheless I do not despair of being
fortunate one day. Meanwhile, it would be a
great consolation to me, if I may so flatter myself, if you would grant me a corner in your

memory, and honour me with your friendship, since I shall never cease to be (etc. . . .).

My most humble respects to Madame your wife and I embrace tenderly my dear god-daughter and the rest of your dear family ; my compliments, if you please, to all our friends of both sexes.

X

You will find from the letter that I am sending herewith to my mother that I have received the honour of yours of the 18th ult.

Permit me to convey my thanks more particularly by these lines, and I beg of you to continue giving me from time to time your dear news when I am travelling in this country, for you cannot know what interest and satisfaction it gives me. You have only to address the letters always to Mr. Joseph Smith, Banker, at Venice (as I mentioned before) who will forward them to me at the different places where I shall be in Italy.

You can well imagine, my very honoured brother, my contentment at learning that you and your dear family are in perfect health, and I wish you with all my heart that you may so continue. To think that I shall embrace you soon gives me real joy. You will do me the justice of believing that. I assure you that this has been one of the principal motives for my undertaking this journey with so much pleasure.

I hope that my desires may be accomplished about next July. Meanwhile I hope that you may have all prosperity, and, giving my compliments to Madame your wife and embracing your dear family, I am, Sir, (etc. . . .).

XI

Since I had the honour of writing to you, ways have been found of engaging Sgra. Merighi, and as she is a contralto it would suit us at present that the woman to be engaged in Italy should be a soprano. I am also writing to this effect to Mr. Swinny by the same post and recommending that the woman he suggests to you should be able to play men's parts as well as women's. I understand that you have not yet engaged a woman contralto, but if you have things must stay as they are.

I take the liberty of asking you again that there should be no mention in the contracts as to first, second or third rôles because that upsets us in the choice of Drama and causes great inconvenience. We also hope with your assistance to get a man and a woman for next season which begins in October this year and ends in July 1731 and we look forward with impatience to news from you in order to inform the Court.

It only remains for me to reiterate my assurances of my particular obligation to you for your goodness towards me in this matter, and

I have the honour to be with respectful affection
(etc. . . .).

XII

I have just received the honour of your letter
of the 22 ult. (new style), from which I learn the
reasons which determined you to engage Sr.
Senesino at fourteen hundred guineas, to which
we agree ; and I thank you humbly for the
trouble you have been to in this affair. The said
Sr. Senesino has arrived here some twelve days
and I did not fail to pay him, on the presentation
of your letter, the hundred guineas on account
of his salary which you promised him. As for
Sigra Pisani, we have not had her, and as the
season is well advanced and the operas are
beginning soon, we will do without another
woman from Italy this year, having arranged
the operas for the company which we at present
have.

I am, however, very much obliged to you for
thinking of Sigra Madalena Pieri, in case another
woman who can do men's parts should become
an absolute necessity ; but we shall remain con-
tent with five people, having actually found
substitutes for the rest.

It is largely owing to your generous assistance
that the Court and the Nobility have at present
a company to their liking, so that it only remains
for me to express to you my particular feelings
of gratitude and to assure you of the very respect-

ful attentions with which I have the honour to be, Sir, (etc. . . .).

XIII

I have received your esteemed letter of January 6, from which I note among other things the care that you have taken in burying my Mother according to her last wishes. I cannot stop my tears here. But it has pleased the Highest thus and I submit to His Holy Will with Christian resignation. But her memory will always stay by me, until we are united after this life, which I hope the Good God may grant us through His mercy.

For the constant loyalty and care with which you helped my mother I will with deeds as well as with words show my gratitude.

I hope that you received in reply to yours of December 28 (old style) my last letters containing enclosures for Herrn Consistorialrat Franck and cousin Diaconus Taust. I am looking forward to your reply, with a note added of the expenses, including the printed Parentalia and Leichen Carmina. Meanwhile I am much obliged for the last magnificent Carmen which you sent and which I shall keep as a highly treasured memorial.

I also condole with you, my brother, and your esteemed wife from my heart, for the great loss that you have suffered through the death of your brother-in-law and I am especially moved by your Christian submission. May the Highest grant us all the realisation of your good wishes, and I recommend you, my esteemed brother, and all your family to His all-powerful protection, and with every submission I remain (etc. . . .).

XIV

I see from the letter which you did me the honour to write me on July 12 (new style) in reply to my last, and by the specification which you added to it, to what pains you were at on the occasion of my very dear Mother's burial.

I am much obliged to you for the copies of the Funeral oraisons which you sent me and to which you wanted to have one added for my dear father ; . . . Mr. Sbüelen.

I shall partly repay the obligations which I owe to you later. Meanwhile I beg you to give my respects and compliments to Madame your dear wife, to my dear god-daughter and to the rest of your dear family and to be very sure yourself that I am, (etc. . . .).

XV

I received your esteemed letter of last month with the enclosure from our dear relations in Gotha, to which I reply by this post. With all my heart I am glad that they and all their dear relations are so well and I wish that they may constantly remain so. Again I see what great pains you have taken with regard to the receipts and expenditure from July 1 last year 1732, to July 30, 1733, over the house which my mother left and I must mention my deep gratitude to you for it.

You mention that it would be necessary for me to see the house myself, but, much as I would like to visit you, I must abstain from such a pleasure owing to pressing affairs, but I will give you my written opinion on it.

It was very good of you, my honoured brother, to remember my mother's last wish regarding her tombstone, and I hope that you will carry it out.

I see from the accounts you sent that Frau Händelin, who lives in the house, pays 6 Reichstaler a year rent; I would like her in future not to pay anything and she can stay there as long as she likes. Herewith I return the account with my signature as desired and I shall not forget my obligations in this respect. My humblest greetings to your dear wife. Kindly greetings to the esteemed Taust family and all our dear friends. I shall soon be a nuisance to you again, but I hope to be pardoned, as I know you and your kindness; I beg you to believe that I shall remain all my life in sincere affection (etc. . . .).

XXI

Since there is no one closer to my heart than my dear niece whom I have always wholly loved, you could not have sent me anything more agreeable than the news that she is to marry a person of such merit and so distinguished a character. Your decision alone would have been sufficient to transport her to the greatest heights of happiness, and I therefore take it as a sign of your consideration that you should ask for my approbation. Her good education, for which she is indebted to you, will not only assure her happiness, but will subscribe also to your consolation, to which you may have no doubt I will do all that I can.

I have taken the liberty of sending to her husband a small wedding present in the form of a gold watch of Delharmes, a gold chain and two seals, one of amethyst and one of onyx. Allow me to send at the same time as a small wedding present to my dear niece, a diamond ring containing a single stone weighing something over seven grains, flawless and of the first water.

I shall address both to Mr. Sbüelen at Hamburg to keep them for you. My obligations to you, Sir, and to your wife, to whom pray give my respects, are another thing, of which I shall endeavour to acquit myself at the first opportunity. Allow me to assure you that there cannot be greater sincerity or more unchanging devotion than I have for you, dear Sir, and very honoured brother (etc. . . .).

XXXI

I was just about to start from the Hague for London when your very agreeable letter was given me by Mr. Passerini. I just had the time to hear his wife sing. Your protection and recommendation sufficed to excite my curiosity, and I must show her my great approbation, for I was soon convinced of her rare merit. They are going to Scotland to fulfil some engagements for concerts for a season of six months. There she could perfect herself in the English Language, and then (since they have the intention to stay for a while in London) I shall not fail to render them any service they need from me.

I was very touched by your polite remarks full of friendship. Your obliging manners and your reputation have made a great impression in my heart and in my mind, and I shall always reciprocate your kindness. Rest assured that you will always find in me sincerity and true esteem.

I thank you for the beautiful work " du sisteme d'intervalles " which you have kindly sent me, it is worthy of your occupation and of your knowledge.

I congratulate you on your perfect state of health which you are enjoying at a fairly advanced age and I wish you with all my heart the continuation of all sorts of prosperity for several years to come. If your Passion for exotic plants could prolong your days and sustain the vivacity that is natural to you, I offer myself with great pleasure to contribute to it in some manner. I therefore make you a present, and I send you (by the enclosed address) a case of flowers; I am told by the connoisseurs of plants that they are choice flowers and of a charming rarity; if what they say is true, you will have the best plants in all England, the season being still proper for having flowers. You will be the best judge of them, I await your decision hereon. Meanwhile don't let me wait too long a time for your agreeable reply to this, for I am with the greatest friendship (etc. . . .).

XXXII

It is some time ago that I had a supply of exotic plants prepared to send to you, when Jean Carsten the Captain (who was told to let you have them), sent news to me that he had heard that you were dead. You will not doubt that this news afflicted me extremely. You can imagine my joy therefore on hearing that you are in perfect health; the same Captain Jean Carsten who has just arrived from your neighbourhood, sends me this good news through a friend, and since you have drawn out a list of exotic plants to procure for you, I take advantage of this opportunity with greatest pleasure. I endeavoured to find these plants, and you will have them almost all; since Captain Carsten need not leave here till the month of December, he has kindly offered to send them by the first boat which leaves here, and on the enclosed slip of paper you will find the name of the captain and the boat. I hope that the little present which I dare offer you will be agreeable to you ; I beg you to give me news of the state of your health, which I hope is perfect, and I also wish you all sorts of prosperity and I am (etc. . . .).

SOURCES

No. 1. Autograph. Unknown. Source : Johann Mat-theson, *Lebensbeschreibung*, Hamburg 1761.

No. 2. Autograph. Unknown. Source : *Letters by several eminent persons deceased. Including the correspondence of John Hughes, Esq., and several of his friends, published from the Originals.* London 1772.

No. 3. Autograph. British Museum, London.

No. 4. Autograph. Formerly in the collection of Fillon, Paris.

No. 5. Autograph. Unknown. Source : Johann Mat-theson, *Critica musica*, Hamburg 1725.

No. 6. Autograph. Unknown. Source : G. F. Handel, *Suites de pièces pour le Clavecin*, London 1720.

No. 7. Autograph. Unknown. Source : G. F. Handel, *Radamisto*, London 1720.

No. 8. Autograph. Archives of Parliament, London.

No. 9. Autograph. Formerly in the collection of Dr. Senff, Calbe/Saale.

No. 10. Autograph. Formerly in the collection of Dr. Senff, Calbe/Saale.

No. 11. Autograph. The collection of Karl Geigy-Hagenbach, Zürich.

No. 12. Autograph. Sacred Harmonic Society, London.

No. 13. Autograph. Formerly in the collection of Dr. Senff, Calbe/Saale. (The autograph is damaged, as Frau Professor Senff cut out Handel's name to present it to the well-known singer Henriette Händel-Schütz (1772-1849).)

No. 14. Autograph. Formerly in the collection of Dr. Senff, Calbe/Saale.

No. 15. Autograph. The collection of Dr. Ernst Foss, Berlin.

No. 16. Autograph. Formerly in the collection of Ch. Salomon, London.

No. 17. Autograph. In the collection of W. Westley Manning, Esq.

No. 18. Autograph. Formerly in the collection of Pölchau, Hamburg. Source : Mattheson, *Grundlage einer Ehrenpforte*, Hamburg 1740.

No. 19. Autograph. The collection of Earl Howe, London.

No. 20. Autograph. Victoria and Albert Museum, London.

No. 21. Autograph. The collection of Dr. Ernst Foss, Berlin.

No. 22. Autograph.
No. 23. Autograph.
No. 24. Autograph.
No. 25. Autograph. The collection of Earl Howe,
No. 26. Autograph.   London.
No. 27. Autograph.
No. 28. Autograph.
No. 29. Autograph.

No. 30. Autograph. British Museum, London.

No. 31. Autograph.
No. 32. Autograph. University Library, Dorpat.

No. 33. Autograph. Royal College of Music, London.

INDEX